ALASKA

D1627306

BERING
SEA

PRIBYLOF
ISLANDS

757 MILES - 6 DAYS.

DUTCH HARBOUR.

ATTU.

ALEUTIAN ISLANDS

1732 MILES - 20 DAYS.

NORTH

PACIFIC OCEAN

TRACK OF THE "TAI-MO-SHAN"

Robert McGown

Desmond McC Dixon

From P.A. + A.A.

$$\frac{27}{\times 11}{49}$$

The Voyage of the Tai-Mo-Shan

Photograph by Robin Adler

THE AUTHOR IN 1946

THE VOYAGE OF THE
TAI-MO-SHAN

By

MARTYN SHERWOOD

GEOFFREY BLES
FIFTY-TWO DOUGHTY STREET
LONDON

PRINTED IN GREAT BRITAIN BY
LOWE AND BRYDONE PRINTERS LTD.
LONDON

First Published March 1935
Reprinted October 1939
Reprinted November 1942
Reprinted November 1946

FOREWORD

It is hoped that this book will prove useful as a guide
and an encouragement to other small-boat owners
who decide to put their dreams into practice. It is more
especially for the latter that the Appendices following
the story of *Tai-Mo-Shan's* voyage are included.

For literary style no merit is claimed, but were one to
hesitate to write on that score alone, surely there would
be fewer of those fascinating book-shops where you and
I have elbowed each other as we greedily glanced
through the new arrivals.

M. B. S.

DROMINAGH, IRELAND,
August, 1934.

CONTENTS

CHAPTER I

Planning the Voyage

In the Spring of 1932 a party of five naval officers serving in the British China Squadron met and talked over the possibilities of sailing home from China to England. Some months before this the project had been thought of but nothing very definite arranged. There were difficulties to be overcome which seemed to us almost insurmountable.

The first thing that had to be done was to get the necessary leave from the naval authorities. Each member of the party had therefore to approach his Commanding Officer and explain the merits of his proposal. The five members of the party were Lieutenant Ryder, Lieutenant Francis and Lieutenant Salt, all serving in submarines, Surgeon-Lieutenant Ommanney-Davis of the sloop H.M.S. *Bridgewater*, and lastly myself of the aircraft-carrier *Hermes*, where I was doing my "big-ship" period of two years from submarines, in which I was also a specialist. The party thus formed consisted of four submarine officers and one naval surgeon. The first three were twenty-four, the doctor twenty-seven and I myself thirty-two years old.

Ryder possessed a limited knowledge of ocean-sailing, having taken part in the Fastnet and Santander races on several occasions, and from the start we all agreed that he should be the sailing-master. Our choice was a good one, and on arrival home he was chosen to command the schooner which is taking Rymill's expedition to the Antarctic.

Francis agreed to study wireless, a subject of which we all had only a very limited knowledge. His subsequent success with our sets on board *Tai-Mo-Shan* will be recounted later. He also took a large number of the photographs in this book, using a Leica camera for the purpose. He shared his watches with the doctor.

Ommanney-Davis was away up in northern waters during the preparations for the trip, and he was not in the least perturbed when he found that he had only two or three days at Hong-Kong in which to buy his kit, etc., before the start. His professional activities were fortunately not needed to any very large extent during the voyage, but, like the rest of us, he kept his watches in addition to his medical duties.

Salt was one of those people who are always on the look-out for some original form of adventure and was in fact one of the founders of this expedition. He had a big burden from the start, as it was on his shoulders that the responsibility lay for keeping the expenses as low as possible. The different currencies experienced and the desire on everybody's part to buy something more made this no easy task. He was also the bo'sun and controlled the supply and consumption of all the hundred-and-one articles that are required for a sailing-vessel putting to sea for a long voyage. He and I formed the starboard watch.

I was most fortunate to be in the party, as I was some years senior to the remainder who asked me to join them. This stamped the expedition with the right spirit from the start, and to show my keenness to take part I readily accepted and volunteered to do the cooking, a post which is not always easy to fill under such strenuous conditions.

Having introduced you to the five young officers who formed the crew of the *Tai-Mo-Shan*, I will let you into the secret of our preparations for the start. Our chief difficulty was one which has always racked the wits of youth, the raising of the necessary money. I do not propose to tell you how this was done ; suffice it to say that even this problem was finally solved. Most of the early stages were spent at Hong-Kong, where, in the evenings aboard one of the ships to which we belonged, five rather earnest young officers would retreat to a suitable cabin to discuss and plan the future.

In the China fleet the movements of ships are regulated primarily by the ever-changing political situation. However, when there is no special insurrection involving British subjects and property, ships move up north to Wei-Hai-Wei as soon as the weather begins to get unpleasantly hot down south. Such was the case in 1932, and so that summer we found ourselves together at this charming summer resort. By this time our applications had been forwarded through our respective Captains to the Commander-in-Chief of the China Station. Finally Admiralty approval was received and we were free to start building a boat.

Now it was not entirely for pleasure that this voyage was being planned. We wanted, if possible, to combine business with pleasure. When we submitted our proposed route it differed slightly from the one which we actually followed. We added a comprehensive letter in which we explained that we were eager to collect meteorological data, information *re* currents and winds experienced, and any other details of a similar nature which might prove useful. Added to this we felt that the experience gained would serve us in good stead at a later date.

Quite rightly, we were placed on half-pay for the entire voyage, and it is amusing to reflect that four of the five members were only receiving about seven shillings a day in consequence.

The comparative ease with which we got the leave was largely due to the encouragement given from the start by Admiral Sir Howard Kelly, K.C.B., and our respective Captains. Even an official document was forwarded with the final clause that " it is refreshing to note this spirit of initiative and adventure." This was distinctly encouraging.

Before leaving Hong-Kong two persons had been approached who were to play a very important part in our preparations. One was Mr. Cock, the Managing Director of the Hong-Kong and Whampoa Dock Company, and the other was Mr. Rouse, the Vice-Commodore of the Royal Hong-Kong Yacht Club. This Dock Company, though it does a very brisk business both building and repairing steamships of every size and description, did not then go in for the construction of ocean-going yachts such as the one that we required. However, Mr. Cock, being himself a keen yachtsman, readily consented to build whatever we demanded. Our next object was to design the vessel and, though we had formulated many ideas by this time, it needed someone with a lot more technical knowledge than we possessed. Mr. Rouse was our man and, though a busy man in Hong-Kong, he scarcely got the opportunity to decline.

The designs were soon taking shape, but each item which needed discussion had to be put to paper and sent to one of us at Wei-Hai-Wei, 1200 miles away. Then another hurried meeting would be called, and back would go the approval or amendment, as the case might be. Thus, in a growing fever of impatience, we passed the summer.

Some of us went down to Shanghai in October. This is one of the gayest cities in the Orient, or anywhere else for that matter, so we had a very enjoyable time. But it was here that our imagination was fired by a visit we paid to a Ningpo junk which was then fitting out at Shanghai for a world-cruise. These junks are provided with ample accommodation, and in this case her captain, who was an art expert, had her fitted out as a travelling art-gallery. There was ornate woodwork everywhere, with rare Ningpo wood-carvings and soapstone art. Despite the fact that one of the local papers said, " They all agree the voyage is safe and as good as over now," I am afraid that the vessel was no more by the time we ourselves reached Formosa, where she was wrecked.

The designs of the boat were finally completed by the end of October, and can be studied in detail in Appendix I. By the middle of November the Dock Company had started work on her. The aircraft-carrier in which I was then serving happened to be dry-docked a few yards from the shed in which *Tai-Mo-Shan* was to take shape. I can still recall the frequent visits which we paid to the scene, though as yet there was not much to show. I think that even those of my readers who have not actively indulged in building a boat for their own purposes will realise the tremendous feeling of suppressed excitement which overcomes one at this period.

There were various types of wood to be collected and big timbers started to arrive daily. China fir for the masts, teak for the hull, camphor-wood and ipol for the frames, and yacal for the stern post. Apart from the preparations necessary for the building of the boat we now turned to the question of getting ourselves " ready in all respects for sea." We had all been busy profiting by the experience of others, and had collected a library of books by ocean-voyagers such as Slocum, Voss, Stock, O'Brien, Robinson and Pidgeon—to name but a few.

We were all down at Hong-Kong for the greater part of the winter, and most of the naval exercises were taking place in the vicinity, which suited our purpose admirably. One of our party, the doctor, was still up north at Chinwantao, where the Japanese and Chinese troubles were then at their height. Later on we were to hear many stories from him about this period. Golf was occasionally disturbed by the dropping of stray bombs. The caddies, in addition to the clubs, carried arms in case of sudden attack. However, he never disclosed whether these rather alarming conditions tended to decrease his handicap or the reverse.

From now until our final departure from Hong-Kong we all worked hard. Even the calm of our designer was once slightly upset by our constant suggestions, and he remarked one day that we must remember that he had got a job in Hong-Kong apart from yacht-designing.

Many were the consultations held long after working hours between the designer, the dock representatives and ourselves. However, as far as we were concerned, most of this part of the preparations was attended to by Ryder, the one member of our party who had previously sailed in boats of this type. The rest of us nevertheless were full of suggestions.

One item which for a day-trip is quite a small detail looms very much larger when it comes to arranging a long ocean voyage. I refer to the cooking problem. After all, it must readily be conceded that it would be somewhat monotonous to live on boiled eggs for the best part of a year! We decided that we ought to get busy about this at once, and so it came about that one day the following appeared in the *South China Morning Post*, under TUITION WANTED : "GENTLEMAN requires COOKING LESSONS evenings four to six." This had rather different results from anything that we had hoped for, since it caught the eye of the director of the Hong-Kong and Shanghai Hotel Company, and he at once enquired into its origin. Through his invitation I had to go through the nerve-racking procedure of an interview with him in his spacious office, first announcing my business by saying that I had come about the cooking. The results exceeded our wildest expectations. There was a Swiss gentleman in charge of the cooking arrangements at the largest hotel in Hong-Kong, and it was to his care that Salt and I were entrusted. He at once sensed that it would be more advantageous for us to be able to boil a potato satisfactorily than produce a Lobster Meunière! The first evening on which we spent our spare time in cooking will indeed live in our memory. White hats and coats were readily provided by our instructor, but the aprons were only sufficient covering for the front. In consequence, therefore, it was not surprising that our back view, which revealed our plus-fours, quite broke down the Oriental calm of the sixty Chinese cooks among whom we were to work for many evenings !

We soon learned sufficient to produce meals varying daily, without relying entirely on tinned foods, so our time was well spent, and we began to regard ourselves as first-class cooks, though it is doubtful whether the others did so after the first trial. Our big mainstay was a pressure-cooker which claimed to do marvellous things, such as cooking a whole meal in one. Our first trial took place aboard one of the Hong-Kong Yacht Club's cruisers, at the end of a Sunday afternoon's race. For this important trial two chickens and a quantity of vegetables were to be cooked. The whistle, which denotes the completion of the cooking, attracted several yachtsmen from other boats, who peered anxiously into our cockpit. You can imagine our feelings when we searched among the vegetables in vain. We later discovered the two chickens which we had omitted to put in the cooker !

There were other duties, apart from the building of the boat, with which we decided to become acquainted before leaving Hong-Kong. One of the most important of these was wireless, as we decided to take this more seriously than is usually the case in small yachts. Francis took over the job. He decided to go in for transmitting as well as receiving. The Amateur Transmitting Society of Hong-Kong were most enthusiastic, and certainly without their aid the transmitter would not have been so well-constructed as it was. It was also tested ashore before installation, and our operator was put through his paces.

A most tricky but necessary job on a trip of this nature is the care of the cash. It is so extraordinarily easy to spend freely when the money belongs to a common fund and does not come directly from one's own pocket. With one owner and unlimited capital this difficulty does not arise. In our case there were five owners and a fixed capital. With the fitting-out of the boat this became very difficult to control. It took a deal of juggling with figures, and it even meant that an interest had to be taken in the fluctuations of the Hong-Kong dollar.

We were fortunate enough to have Ommanney-Davis, the surgeon, in our crew, and so we were able to leave the responsibility for all medical stores entirely in his hands. Though, as the account of the voyage will show, the health of the crew was extraordinarily good, a great deal of the medical stores were later on to prove invaluable to the natives of Attu in the Aleutian Islands, and to those of Crooked Island in the Bahamas.

To give a list of all the stores which we had to get ready would not only fill too much space but would weary the patience of the reader. However, to give some idea of the work that had to be done, here are a few items :

> Boatswain's Stores,
> Navigational Instruments,
> Electrical Equipment,
> Wireless Equipment,
> Photographic Equipment,
> Fishing and Shooting Equipment,

Personal Clothing,
Medical Stores,
Crockery and Cooking Utensils,
50 Gallons of Kerosene,
270 Gallons of Fresh Water,
100 days' supply of Dry Provisions.
Etc.

The dimensions of the boat were as follows : Displacement 23½ tons, length 54 feet overall and 42 feet designed water-line. Her draft was 8 feet 5 inches, and in ketch rig she had a sail area of 1,040 square feet. Her extreme beam was 12 feet 2½ inches, with a beam on the water-line of 10 feet 11½ inches.

And so our boat reached the final stages in what seemed to her future owners quite a short time.

CHAPTER II

Tai-Mo-Shan

A big advantage which, as a matter of fact, we had not foreseen, was the fact of having the designer actually on the spot. In half-an-hour's interview we found that most of the outstanding difficulties could be discussed. Such was the case during the building, when alterations and adjustments were frequently necessary.

Our time for the voyage was limited by the fact that we had, of course, to resume naval duties on arrival home. We wanted, in consequence, a boat which, while being comparatively fast, would at the same time be sufficiently seaworthy to ride out the worst of gales. As can be seen from the plans, the designer produced a vessel of exceptional grace and beauty. After sailing in her some 16,000 miles, I can say with confidence that she proved as good as she looks. We never regretted our decision for ketch rig, though I prefer to champion this cause elsewhere, lest at this early stage I annoy those who are not in agreement with me.

By the middle of April the boat had progressed so favourably that she was then moved out of the shed in which she had been built and, when we weighed her, we found that she was about one ton less than we had expected. This was a great joy, as it meant that we had that amount to play with on other fittings and stores.

On St. George's Day she first floated in her native element. I expect a good many small-boat owners have wondered, as we did, whether she would turn turtle or merely lie on her side. Actually, she floated to her marks.

We now had to choose a name. This was done by the process of elimination, and we finally decided on the most suitable of several Chinese names connected with the place of her birth. "Tai-Mo-Shan" is the name of the highest mountain in Hong-Kong, and though boasting no special attraction in the way of scenery, is a favourite week-end climb for those who have their business in that town. The literal translation of the name is High Hat Hill. I am afraid that no launching ceremony took place. There were several reasons for this. Our main object was to avoid publicity as much as possible. Some time previously a Chinese junk had been manned by a party of young men with similar ideas to our own. For reasons of which I am not aware they only covered some few days' voyage from Hong-Kong, to which they then returned for good. We were therefore viewed with a little suspicion by those favoured few who were in the know.

Other considerations of a more important nature compelled a rather hush-hush policy. Not more than a few miles from Hong-Kong is Bias Bay, the notorious lair of Chinese pirates. To the average person in England or America who has not visited Chinese waters the mention of pirates brings visions of the Spanish Main and rich cargoes of gold bullion and plate. In China to-day piracy is still a very real menace to coastal shipping. It is certainly no casual venture, but is so highly organised and planned beforehand as to make success almost a foregone conclusion.

On the 7th January, 1933, a Danish steamer, the *Gustav Diederichen*, was pursuing her course from Hong-Kong to Swatow. It was ten o'clock in the forenoon, and she had gone but a few miles when several of her recently-embarked passengers held up the officers with revolvers. They had taken advantage of the foggy weather then prevailing, and so well-timed was their attack that a Chinese junk arrived on the scene according to plan. To this vessel three of the richer Chinese passengers were forced to transfer and to accompany their captors, while the steamship proceeded to inform the naval authorities of her miserable plight. The chief engineer had been wounded by a revolver-shot. Unfortunately, by the time the authorities were informed, both the pirates and their miserable victims were well inland in Chinese territory at the rear of Bias Bay. A handsome ransom would be required, and a date given for its payment. Should the latter fall due and no money be forthcoming, what could be more simple than the despatch of an ear or a finger to serve as a small but telling reminder?

It was not because we thought that we were worth anything in hard cash, but because we felt that these gentlemen might think us so, that we purposely avoided publishing more information about our plans than we considered necessary. I think that we would have held our own against a Chinese junk, though, had she chanced upon us unawares under cover of darkness; it would have been an interesting encounter for the twentieth century. Their cannon are very antiquated pieces, while our main armament was a harpoon-gun with several 12-bore shot-guns as secondary armament. I think this order suits their effectiveness !

By the first week in April *Tai-Mo-Shan* had progressed so well that we were favoured with a visit by the new Commander-in-Chief of the China Station, Admiral Sir Frederick Dreyer, K.C.B., C.B.E., who had recently relieved Admiral Sir Howard Kelly, G.B.E., K.C.B., etc.

It was an exceptionally hot and sticky morning when we arrived on board the flagship H.M.S. *Kent*. The five of us were summoned to the Admiral's cabin, where we explained our proposed route. I mention this interview, as it had a direct bearing on the route which we were to take. One of the places which we had intended to visit was Ganges Island. Its position is reckoned as some 850 miles to the eastward of Yokohama. Its very existence is doubtful, but from time to time it is reported by ships. The following is an extract from the *Pacific Ocean Pilot*, Vol. 1, 1924 :

" Ganges Island : (Lat. 30° 47′ N., 154° 15′ E.)— about 390 miles northward of Minami Tori Shima—is one of the many dangers that have been reported in this locality at various times, but nothing positive is known as to its proper position, although numerous reports point to the fact of the probable existence of some danger in this region, the establishment of which is important.

" Reef : A reef is reported to lie about 8 miles to the northward of Ganges Island. In view of the uncertainty of the position of Ganges Island the locality must be navigated with caution.

" In 1911 the ss. *Winnabago* passed over the assigned

position of Ganges Island without observing any indication of its existence."

The following extract is published in the supplement to the above publication, correcting it to August 1931 :

" In consequence of a recent unsuccessful search by a Japanese Government vessel for Ganges Island and the reef northward of it, during which soundings of 3,000 fathoms were obtained in the vicinity of their charted positions, the existence of this Island and reef is considered to be doubtful, and they have been marked ' E.D.' [1] on the charts."

Now, though the Admiral did not wish to issue orders regarding our route, since our whole voyage was an unofficial expedition, he made it pretty clear that, with the typhoon season approaching, he considered this part of the trip would prove more perilous than useful. We deferred to his wishes and, though we did not show it, were rather relieved at cutting out what had constituted one of the excuses for our expedition in our original plan.

The Admiral inspected *Tai-Mo-Shan*, and as the fleet were shortly moving up to North China, he took this opportunity of bidding us goodbye. Before doing so, however, he said that he hoped we would get away as soon as possible, before the start of the typhoon season.

The interest taken on this occasion stimulated both our dockyard friends and ourselves to a pitch of energy which lasted right up to the day of our departure.

On St. George's Day, the 23rd April, as I have previously mentioned, *Tai-Mo-Shan* proudly floated in the waters of Hong-Kong.

[1] Existence Doubtful.

From now on everything was more exciting than it had been to date. The Dock Company had constructed the major portion of the fittings in their various workshops, so that it was surprising how quickly she began to look like the finished article. We were, all this time, having a friendly rivalry with two Americans, Messrs. Kilkenny and Thomson, who were constructing a vessel for themselves at a Chinese yard. As we both started at about the same time, it gave us an added impetus. They had suffered a stroke of bad luck when the mould burst which was to take the lead for their keel, and the metal, about 8 tons of it, ran down into the sea. Chinamen being, however, great economists, were not to be defeated so easily, and when we left some two months later, a Chinese labourer was still busy chipping the metal out of the rocks. Our own 7-ton keel looked a massive affair. It was cast in one of the shops and bolted on.

We had, of course, numerous ideas on details of construction which we were convinced were necessary in the production of a perfect ocean-sailing yacht ; many of these ideas were incorporated in *Tai-Mo-Shan's* design, and I will enumerate some of them.

We had decided on Bermuda rig, and though this requires a tall mast in order to obtain the required sail area, we found that *Tai-Mo-Shan* needed only a 52-ft. mast for our comparatively small sail area with her lightly-driven hull. We fitted roller-reefing gear, by means of which in the roughest weather one man was able to reef down the mainsail. Though one objection to roller-reefing is that the sails are liable to be pulled out of shape, our working sails were of 8-oz. cotton duck, which probably accounts for their excellent shape at the end of our voyage.

The fitting of a breakwater, which was possibly the outcome of " naval training," later proved invaluable, not only as a protection to people working around the mast but also to gear stowed on the upper deck. Abaft this breakwater we were able to lash our collapsible canvas boat on the port-side, while on the starboard-side it served as protection to the sea-anchors and 4-inch warp.

I think the fact that four of us were submarine officers had a great bearing on the design of the fore-hatch. This was a massive galvanised affair clamping down on a rubber seating. It ensured complete water-tightness up for'ard, an object seldom attained in wooden yachts.

In most yachts of over 20 tons it is usual to steer with a wheel. The fact that we had a tiller was one of the first things remarked on by people who were paying their first visit to the vessel. We found in later experience that steering even in the roughest weather was comparatively easy on such a perfectly-balanced boat. It has the added advantage of being so simple ; since there is no gearing to strip or wire to break, and with a lanyard the shocks can be quite easily controlled when the rudder is jerking badly in rough weather. The sense of " feel " of how the boat is sailing is imparted by a tiller, so as to provide endless satisfaction and confidence to the helmsman.

The steering was achieved from a cockpit of minimum size and some eighteen inches in depth, which not only gave added accommodation below but also ensured the minimum amount of water being embarked in the event of being "pooped." As it was self-draining, it caused us no worry. In fact, seated behind a permanent wooden dodger which served also as a protection for meteorological instruments, one could enjoy great protection. A movable canvas dodger could be easily erected in addition, where most required.

Between decks we were determined to have as much ventilation as possible, and we gave much thought to this point in her design. In most yachts, when in harbour, with the fore-hatch and skylight open one can ensure a good flow of air through the boat. At sea, when the lop necessitates the closing of the fore-hatch, and very often the skylight as well, the air remains undisturbed, and it is not very long before the atmosphere becomes pretty heavy. As there was every prospect of several weeks on end to be spent at sea, we decided to achieve some form of ventilation which could remain open whatever the weather might be. Instead of a skylight, which is apt to leak, we had removable cowls, which, in rough weather, could be replaced by screw-in glass caps. Up in the starboard rigging we fitted a windsail, which was really nothing more complicated than a length of canvas hose, opened out at its upper end by an iron hoop. The lower end was led down through the deck abreast the mast, where it joined into a metal trunking inside the boat. In this manner the air was conveyed to the for'ard end, so that we were always ensured of a small flow through the boat.

We had planned to go well north into latitudes where we could reasonably expect it to be really cold. In order to combat this we purchased an ordinary household "Demon" stove, which burned kerosene. The heat from this stove could also be diverted through the bulkhead by means of a deflector into quite a spacious cupboard. This we used for drying our clothes. The exhaust was led away by means of a trunking at the top of this compartment to an exhaust cowl on the cabin roof. That stove certainly had to do a lot, for apart from both these heating and drying activities, it proved most useful as an alternative cooking-stove.

The internal arrangements of *Tai-Mo-Shan* were somewhat unorthodox, since everything was laid out to accommodate five men. There was enough for us, but the addition of one other would have thrown the whole expedition out of joint and entailed serious re-arrangements of design. Even from the number of bunks down to the number of knives and forks, five was the number allowed for.

Our fresh-water supply came from six tanks which were situated under the deck of the saloon, and it was a simple matter to pump it up into suitably-situated ready-use tanks as occasion demanded. The total amount carried was 250 gallons, representing a total weight of just over a ton. We found that one gallon per day per man was an ample allowance where washing was not considered to be quite such an important function as modern convention would have it.

The question of having an engine was fully discussed. Our decision against it was greatly influenced by the question of weight. Not only does it add weight, but, together with fuel, an engine takes up a considerable amount of space. Also, in the interests of some members of the party who were only just managing to raise the necessary funds, the exchequer was being most jealously guarded by the member whose responsibility it was that we should set off with something in the bag.

In most cases, when the internal lay-out of a yacht is being decided, the cook has no say in the matter, and so, more often than not, the galley is stuffed away up in the forward end of the boat. Here the motion is the worst and the ventilation least. In our case, with no paid cook, I myself took a more than passing interest in this point. Besides being easier on the cook, the fact of having the galley aft helps to keep the saloon very much cooler and clear of fumes. This was a most important detail on a trip where several months of tropical weather were to be experienced. The cooking-range, which was built at a garage in Hong-Kong, was fitted with two paraffin pressure-stoves, with an oven between them. The whole range was slung on gymbals. But the story of the trip will reveal more about the antics of this piece of furniture than I wish to disclose at present.

The boat was lit throughout by electricity. A 12-volt battery situated under the flooring of the wireless cabinet made this possible. It could be charged by a small $\frac{1}{2}$-horse-power petrol generating plant or a wind-mill dynamo. The latter, when in use, was mounted on deck at the head of the breakwater. This battery served the double purpose of supplying both the electricity for the lights and power for the wireless installation.

By early May 1933 the permanent fittings were completed, and she was at last ready for the eagerly-awaited trial trip.

CHAPTER III

The Start

In Hong-Kong there are several Chinese boat-building firms who have turned out some really well-constructed boats at very reasonable prices. Unfortunately, however, one cannot always rely on the time in which they promise to have a job completed. Should he run out of bronze screws, the chances are that a Chinese workman will finish off the job with steel ones. But, to give him his due, he is an excellent craftsman, his scarfing being of the very highest order. In the case of our vessel, the work of the dockyard labourers was watched by a certain canny Scot. If they ever hoodwinked him I must allow them more credit for cunning than I thought possible. Their wages are phenomenally low, though I expect the day is not far off when the " old order changeth." Their living expenses are extremely small, which is, I think, largely due to the very satisfactory filling propensities of quite a small amount of rice. This can be purchased at very low cost. Their clothes are of the simplest order, while their spare time is spent in such harmless pastimes as taking their favourite caged-bird out for an airing. Even their pipes hold a very small amount of tobacco and would, I think, prove a distinct disadvantage when staying under a friend's roof.

Their wages being in proportion to their living expenses, one can have a boat built there probably cheaper than anywhere else in the world at the present time. Had it not been for these circumstances, it is doubtful whether *Tai-Mo-Shan* could ever have materialised. However, materialise she did, and greatly to our satisfaction. We had again to call on local talent for all the designing of our sails, and here Mr. G. G. Wood, another local yachtsman, solved our troubles. They were made to his design by the Chinese firm of Ah Lung, who have a large sail-loft tucked away in a very crowded part of the Chinese quarter of Hong-Kong. As the Chinaman is of a conservative nature, the sewing-machine was not in use, so that every stitch of our sails was hand-sewn. The complete outfit of sails totalled sixteen, which rather large number was necessary to allow for the varying weather which we were bound to experience.

I do not think that there was one of us who had not under-estimated the amount of work to be done. In addition, a great number of things which were not obtainable in Hong-Kong had to be ordered from England. This meant a delay of at least two months. The Admiralty were good enough to loan us a number of navigational instruments, such as charts, sailing directories, chronometers, and a sextant, etc. We merely had to insure them against damage or total loss. This saved us a great deal of additional expense and made the keeping of meteorological reports, etc., which we had volunteered to do, well worth while. The Marconi Company also loaned us a wireless set, so that with the help of the local amateurs we were well provided for in this respect.

We were doing a great deal of sailing in and around Hong-Kong harbour at this period, in the local cruiser class, and in order to get accustomed to night-sailing, we had some races, in which the younger of the local yachtsmen took part, which started at 7 p.m. They provided us with great amusement, as the Chinese fishing junks seldom carry lights at night. Their presence can frequently be detected, however, by their odour. The local Press began to get interested in our plans, and even the English papers which arrived in Hong-Kong had a brief announcement of our proposed trip. We were very keen to get started, in consequence.

By early May it is getting extremely hot in Hong-Kong, and as we had the prospects of cold weather before us, our wardrobes had to be made up accordingly. Oilskins, sou'-westers, sea-boots, were piled into the boat alongside thick sweaters and underwear; and before we were ready thin cotton shirts and shorts and sun-helmets joined the mixed array. The confusion was almost beyond belief. The Dock Company were working overtime and the boat hummed with activity. The extreme heat down below made the work most difficult, and as everybody considered his own special job quite the most important of the lot, there were times when it became very nearly unbearable. A Chinese carpenter would be fitting up a cupboard; an electrician trying to wire the lights; a joiner trying to make the bilge pump work; one of our party trying to stow away innumerable tins of canned meat; another trying to test out the wireless; and, just to add the final link to the chain of confusion, someone else would be spraying fresh water over the rest of us in his earnest endeavours to fill the tanks. I think, however, the climax was reached one day when the cook arrived down with the leading talent from the local hotel to try out his culinary art on the newly-fitted stove. This included baking bread in the oven.

It was a welcome relief when we set off for our first sail outside Hong-Kong, which was of only four days' duration. It made us realise that it would not be long before we would be settling down to enjoy the fruit of our labours. There was one most amusing incident, when one of the first meals was being prepared. It was noticed that it might suffer if the cook was not given some help, as the motion had completely altered his colouring. His assistant unfortunately becoming over-come in addition, there was an ugly rush by both of them to the bucket, which was fortunately close at hand. However, though this first trip may have discovered some of the weaker points of the crew, there were only a very few alterations to be done to the boat. The bottom had to be coppered, as this is a necessity in tropical waters, where worms can do great damage in a very short space of time. For this purpose *Tai-Mo-Shan* was put into dry-dock and given her final touches.

Our doctor only arrived down from up North a few days before the departure, and a mad rush took place to provide ourselves with passports and all the other official papers without which we could not sail. Not many people knew when we were going, though people began to think we must soon be off. The result was that we were attending dinner-parties and paying bills and embarking stores until it seemed as if we would never be finished. The food with which we started was considered sufficient for one hundred days, and it certainly was ample. The office in which the designs and plans of *Tai-Mo-Shan* were drawn up began to resemble a grocer's shop more and more as the days passed by. And when one saw the amount of provisions stacked there, it seemed impossible to stow so much in such a small space as the boat offered. Provisions alone weighed 1½ tons and occupied a total space in the boat of 174½ cubic feet. There were some large quantities, but very little was subsequently wasted. Of biscuits there were 280 lbs., of tinned beef 144 lbs., of flour 147 lbs., of sugar 100 lbs., of sardines 144 tins, of herrings 72 tins, and of mustard 10 lbs. ! A friend enquired rudely whether we intended taking mustard-baths *en route* ! We always attempted to carry as much fresh stock as possible, so we had to embark in addition 200 oranges, 300 eggs packed in salt, 2 sacks of potatoes, and two sacks of onions. These were but a few of the items. Luckily, we did not forget a tin-opener !

Gradually, with the help of several volunteers, order grew where chaos had previously reigned, and we realised that at last we could make a start. We did not announce our final departure, but intimated that we would not return should our trial be successful.

A few friends joined the staff of the Hong-Kong and Whampoa Dock Company in bidding us farewell, and so, on Wednesday the 31st May, 1933, we were off at last.

CHAPTER IV

Japanese Waters

As soon as we were at sea we eagerly set about our respective duties. Naval rank and seniority were forgotten, and as one of the younger members of the party was the only one who was experienced in sailing this type of boat, he had been unanimously voted as sailing-master of the vessel. As we were all equally efficient navigators by virtue of our profession, we decided that the duties of navigator should also be done by the sailing-master, thus preventing any chance of difficulties arising from too many experts having a hand in it. This left the remaining four members of the crew free to split up the watches and allow time for miscellaneous duties such as wireless, cooking and the repair of gear. Quite a number of people, on hearing of our proposed adventure, had warned us against the dangers of quarrelling amongst ourselves, and it was quite a common thing to be told that we would be scratching each others' eyes out before we had crossed the Pacific. Admittedly, with five people much about the same age, all of whom had spent some considerable time at sea and reckoned that they knew all that there was to be known about seamanship, the possibilities of a fracas looked promising. In fact, the general opinion was that even if we succeeded in reaching home successfully, it would not be with the same five as crew together.

However, among ourselves we did not view the situation quite so seriously. As we had known each other for the past two years, during which time we had had to come to several mutual decisions, we knew each other's failings pretty well and were prepared to make allowances for them accordingly.

Our route was to be rather an unusual one for a sailing-ship. Although the Pacific has been crossed a number of times by small yachts, the route taken has nearly always been from East to West along the attractive South Sea Islands. Here they have the distinct advantage of fair winds. Our object in choosing to go East about was in order to cover fresh ground, as we were all fairly well acquainted with a large portion of the route home *via* the Indian Ocean. In order to achieve our object it was necessary to take a northerly course to avoid the head-winds which we would have encountered had we steered an easterly course from Hong-Kong. These circumstances prompted us to go still farther north and visit the Aleutian Islands.

As Hong-Kong faded out astern we began to wonder why anyone could ever have suggested embarking on such a trip, with all the discomforts attached to it. Of the five of us, three were soon suffering from violent sea-sickness. In a normal year the monsoon has changed to S.W. by this time, but we were still experiencing the north-easterly blow which gave us a horrid bumpy motion on our northerly course. One of our own submarines which was out exercising came over and steered so close that I was forced to hurry down below to avoid them witnessing my early defeat at the hands of the ocean ! I think it was her presence, however, that really brought home to us how lucky we were, despite the discomforts caused by the sea. In the normal course of events one of us should have been in that submarine. Here we were, with nothing to worry us except for the fact that we were to endeavour to reach England by April, and that seemed a long way off then ! Time was our own ; we had no masters ; clothing was mainly conspicuous by its absence, and there was no one to draw attention to the fact that it was wrong to eat your food out of a bowl, with your feet on the table.

Two days out, the N.E. monsoon died away, and for twenty-four hours we were to experience our first calms. Many more were to follow ! These calms were punctuated at intervals by severe rain-squalls accompanied by heavy gusts of wind (about force 8 [1]). We had fitted a klaxon alarm, which was worked electrically from the cockpit and made sufficient noise in the boat to awaken the heaviest of sleepers. By keeping a careful look-out, a warning of the approach of these storms was given and the mainsail was got in before any damage could be done. I think that at this stage we all began to feel that we were in for a more active time than we had anticipated.

However, by Saturday morning the weather cleared and a light wind sprang up from the S.W., heralding the arrival of the monsoon from that direction. By noon on that day we had done 212 miles from Hong-Kong towards the island of Formosa. We could now consider ourselves clear of the attacks of pirates. At

[1] Refers to Beaufort wind-scale, which is given in Appendix VI.

dawn on Sunday we were overtaken by two sub-marines who were on passage to Wei-Hai-Wei from Hong-Kong, and as we had sighted neither the sun nor any land for forty-eight hours, they were able to give us a check on our position. It was disappointing that we were not making better speed when they came up with us.

That same evening the S.W. monsoon started to blow in earnest and continued to increase throughout Sunday night. By Monday morning it was blowing so hard that we were logging $8\frac{1}{2}$ knots. In fact, during the 24 hours preceding our arrival we did 196 miles. As we stood to win champagne should we beat the 200-mark, as a result of a bet before we started, we were in high spirits. Little did we then think that this distance was to remain our best for several months. On Tuesday, 6th June, we had completed the remaining 47 miles and dropped our anchor that evening in the quarantine anchorage of Keelung. This harbour lies at the northernmost end of the Japanese island of Formosa. We had covered 545 miles from Hong-Kong, but despite the short distance we felt a tremendous elation at having arrived at this our first port of call. It had taken us a little over five days, making a daily average of 101 miles. By the surreptitious use of a bucket during the first two or three days I had managed to produce meals for those of the remainder who desired them. It is well worth going through this very unpleasant sensation just to experience the marvellous feeling of exhilaration that takes its place as soon as one has grown accustomed to the motion.

It was not until the following morning that the

Japanese officials began to arrive. Some of us had chosen to sleep on deck, and I am afraid that our guests must have been as surprised to be received by us in pyjamas as we were to have been awakened by the syren of their steam-launch at 6.45 a.m. Even at that very early hour they were most immaculate. There were representatives from the army, the navy, the customs and the medical services. I am afraid their swords must have been extremely uncomfortable aboard so small a vessel. As there were fourteen of them, our saloon was filled to its utmost capacity, and those of the crew sleeping down below got a rather rude awakening. Some of the visitors had a slight command of the English language, which, observing that none of us knew any Japanese, was just as well. They seemed very surprised when, as a result of their enquiries, we explained that we were doing the trip solely for pleasure.

We had agreed amongst ourselves that we would be teetotal while at sea—a rule to which we rigidly adhered throughout our voyage, with the exception of a bottle of wine on the following Christmas evening. Luckily we had on board a few bottles of whisky for just such emergencies as this one. Despite the early hour, these proved extremely acceptable to our guests. Medical and customs formalities occupied some hours and, as more officials joined those on board, we were not anchored in our final billet near the main landing-wharf until well on in the forenoon.

The Mayor of Keelung kindly took us ashore for lunch, and since we had missed our breakfast, we polished off even the dried seaweed. Four of us were afterwards motored up to Taihoku, the chief city, some forty minutes' journey. We had to leave one of the crew on board, so Ryder did not accompany us. We went by train to visit the British Consul at Tam-sui and were accompanied by a member of the police force, presumably to see that we did not get into trouble. At the British Consul's we were warmly welcomed, partly because his wife had recently had two dreams. One of these had already come true, and as in the other she had dreamed that we had been wrecked, she was glad to see us in the flesh. They had reason to be anxious, as only a short time previously they had acted as hosts to the crew of the junk which we had visited up at Shanghai. Apparently, after setting out from Shanghai this vessel encountered blinding rain-squalls and, unable to verify its position, had been dashed to pieces on a wild bit of the coast of Formosa. Now Chinese junks have a wooden eye fixed on their bow. This is to ward off any evil spirit which they may meet with on their voyages. The captain and crew were lucky to escape with their lives, and though the *Fou Po* was a total wreck, their chief concern was that they were unable to recover the money which had been deposited under this eye for good " joss."

Our billet for the night was at an hotel in Taihoku, to which we returned that evening, but our police friend had tired of waiting and we came home unescorted. Next morning things started to move rapidly. We were just in the middle of the first Press interview of our trip with a representative from the *Osaka Times*, when the timely arrival of the Secretary for Foreign Affairs helped us out of our difficulty.

We then had to hurry round somewhat faster than was our usual custom. In one hour we were escorted to make our call on the Governor, and were then shown Government House, a Chinese temple with a magnificently ornate roof, and finally the museum. This all took place in pouring rain. We would like to have been able to spend longer studying the types of head-hunters and various wild tribes who are natives of Formosa. Head-hunting has been put a stop to, but a massacre of some two hundred Japanese took place a few years ago. We could not board our train for Keelung before a flashlight photo had been taken.

Some members of the Japanese Royal Family were shortly visiting the island. As they usually play golf, and the golf course is some way from Taihoku, the roads are re-made for the whole distance. Their visits are therefore greatly welcomed by the golfing members of the foreign community.

When we arrived back at Keelung we found Ryder eager to get to the local bath-house, as while we had been away he had been required to stop on board *Tai-Mo-Shan*. I accompanied him to the bath-house, and while he was removing the stains of the journey I went off elsewhere. I met the policeman who was responsible for the boat. He rushed up very excitedly and enquired as to Ryder's whereabouts, and, as his English was limited, I had no success in my explanations. In any case he must have misunderstood me, for the last I saw of him was rushing off in the direction of the fortifications, to visit which is strictly forbidden to foreign visitors.

As we were setting off in the morning on the next

stage of our journey, we returned to the boat to stow away our laundry, which had been sent aboard by this time. Salt had been the first to arrive, and had already marked a large portion of the clothing with a distinctive tab of brown cotton. The other three had got there just in time to rescue a certain amount, but as I was the last to arrive, I was not left with much. I think, however, it squared out fairly evenly by the end of our voyage !

That evening we gave a reception at the local restaurant to our police friends and others. It could not be called expensive as it only cost fifteen yen (about 15s.). The Japanese waitresses were exceptionally pretty, but one of us had a serious shock. Suddenly one of these girls seemed very excited about our presence there, and from our Japanese friends we discovered that she was sure that I was the man to whom she had lost her heart some years previously. All my protests were of little avail, especially as I, the one concerned, had, to the certain knowledge of the other four, been serving my time on the China Station at the period in question. Even when she produced a photograph-album, it was very difficult to convince her of her error, despite the fact that the picture depicted an able seaman to whom I considered I bore no resemblance.

At noon next day, 8th June, we were kindly given a free tow to the entrance and were loaded down with presents of bananas, melons, onions and potatoes. In the rowing-boat were numerous officials, all in their best uniforms, and military policemen complete with swords. The following day we passed close to Yoko Sima, the most southerly of the Pinnacle Islands. It was early morning and there was a silent grandeur about this island as it loomed out of the mist, and its green-covered slopes were a refreshing sight, but were to be lost to view a short while afterwards. We passed some Japanese fishing-vessels hereabouts.

We had settled down well to the routine by this time and certainly there was no question of quarrelling. I mention this here as in many books it is slurred over or purposely omitted. In *Greenland Days* Martin Lindsay describes the reactions of the various members of the party, both to the existing circumstances and to one another, in a very frank manner. Actually we were all much too occupied to have time to get on one another's nerves.

This is how we spent the twenty-four hours. There were four of us to keep watch, as Ryder was both the navigator and master of the vessel. In order to ensure ample precautions for safety, the other four of us worked watch-and-watch, so that there were always two of us on deck, unless it was absolutely calm weather. All this time we were experiencing very light winds, which entail almost more work for the crew than with a steady wind of stronger force. As soon as the wind fell sufficiently light, we would lower the cruising-sails and replace them with the ballooners. Salt and I formed the starboard watch. We kept the afternoon (noon to 4 p.m.) and the first (8 p.m. to midnight), but Salt alone turned out at 4 a.m. for the morning watch, as I had the duties of cook to perform in addition to my watches. I was called about 6 a.m. to prepare the breakfast. Later on, when I became more efficient, I found I could lie in much later. Ryder, if required, would take my place on deck. The port watch, consisting of Francis and Ommanney-Davis, kept the forenoon (8 a.m. to noon), the first and last dog (4 p.m. to 8 p.m.) and the middle watch (midnight to 4 a.m.). We were therefore kept fully occupied.

The real fireworks began when I turned out, and it usually started the day off well with a good deal of mockery at my expense. We had started off from Hong-Kong with two pressure-stoves which were a cheap copy of the real thing, intended for sale to the unsuspecting Chinese coolies. It was no easy matter to make them function at all, and my relief when they were at last " roaring " was marked by the cessation of unrepeatable language. The conditions were made more complicated by rough weather. First the bottle of methylated spirits would slide off the galley table, to roll down into the bilges, followed by the kerosene. Then, just as the stoves looked like working, they too would follow suit. However, breakfast usually arrived by a quarter-past eight. We demanded good meals, too, for when breathing sea air continually, one is always hungry. Lack of exercise tends to increase rather than diminish the craving for food.

For breakfast we had either porridge, prunes or stewed fruit, followed by various types of egg, usually accompanied by hearty helpings of potato-chips or hot cakes, etc. We had plenty of bread for a time, as this we still considered eatable on the eleventh day after leaving harbour. Some of our friends would have found great amusement in the sight of one of us, clad in a bathing-dress or shorts, scrubbing out the inside of the boat after breakfast. The midday meal was a cold one

which was easily provided, but usually consisted of
fairly substantial amounts of corned-beef, sardines,
salmon or cheese. We carried large quantities of biscuits, which were always welcome. Washing-up was
an evil shared equally by all.

The evening meal got larger as the voyage increased,
as more and more was demanded. At this time it consisted of massive stews with double the quantity of
ingredients allowed for in the cookery-book. Even
at this early stage one of the crew was swearing that he
was going to start " banting." I was trying my hand
at baking, and produced a fairly edible currant scone,
though, the oven being unsatisfactory, I was working
under great difficulties. The drinking-water was then
full of small pieces of wood. It was our fault for not
having seen the ready-use tanks cleaned out properly
before leaving. We were growing quite accustomed
to the shrill whistling of the pressure-cooker. It even
worked as a laundry, which was most convenient for
dish-cloths.

Our spare time was spent in sleeping, and as soon as
one's head was on the pillow one was asleep. This life,
in calm weather, at any rate, proved to be a sure cure
for insomnia. The wireless-operator was becoming
quite expert now, and as he was receiving the weather
reports regularly, we were able to draw out synoptic
charts for that part of the ocean in which we were
sailing. Also, after a little practice, we became pretty
expert at weather-forecasting, and could give a good idea
of what sort of weather conditions we were likely to
expect. The typhoon season in the China seas starts
about the middle of June. These typhoons follow a

more or less regular track. Forming around Yap, an island lying to the eastward of the Philippines, they move over them and into China south of Hong-Kong, where in the early months they fill up and are a menace no longer. As the season advances they curve into China with increasing violence, and sweep out again and across the sea to Japan, where they sometimes do immense damage both to lives and property. The most serious position in which one can be is that area over which the centre of the disturbance is going to pass. The force of the wind reaches as much as 130 miles an hour. As on our passage from Formosa to Yokohama the season was well advanced, we were watching the reception of our weather reports with added interest.

On the twelfth morning after our departure from Keelung we drew near to Yokohama. We had experienced light weather for most of the way, and our best day's run was 170 miles on our second day out, while our average daily run for this leg of the journey was 95. We sailed one thousand one hundred and forty-four miles, which took us twelve days. We got a great thrill as we passed a Japanese battleship and several other smaller men-of-war. We knew we were getting close to our next goal. All the same, the reception outside Yokohama breakwater came as a complete surprise to all of us.

A launch met us with a load of Press representatives and a battery of cameras. While she was escorting us inside to the quarantine anchorage, at least forty carrier-pigeons were released, taking with them numerous photographs and reports. One wonders what on earth they do with them all. We anchored in the quarantine anchorage, and awaited the arrival of the officials to go through the usual formalities.

CHAPTER V

Yokohama

The officials who came to visit us here were very quick in despatching their business and exhibited the usual Japanese courtesy. A little difficulty was experienced, however, owing once more to our complete ignorance of their language and the rather small command of the English language possessed by one of the officials. This official was very keen to interrogate us as to our purpose in going up north, but as he did not understand when we told him that we were going up there for pleasure, we had to put it in some other way to satisfy his determination. Luckily, there was a text book of natural history at hand, and by pointing to pictures in the appropriate section we made him understand that we were a party of learned scientists who were studying botany.

We were given a good anchorage close to the public gardens, and this time we obtained the services of a watchman to look after the boat during our absence. From the moment that we stepped ashore here we realised that by virtue of being naval officers we were going to be looked after very well indeed, and we were at once taken charge of by the obliging agent of the Canadian Pacific Steamship Company. As there are usually some three or four British officers engaged in learning the Japanese language at Tokio, those who were doing so at the time of our arrival were also soon on the spot. We lunched with the British Naval Attaché and his wife at Tokio, and in return invited them back to lunch aboard the boat. As this was our first lunch-party, we were determined to do our best to make it a good one. It took two of us all the previous evening to get the food prepared, and owing to the limited space a certain amount had also to be cooked overnight. I had never expected to see two so-called intelligent naval officers practising the folding of paper serviettes, with a well-known cookery-book to guide them. However, by midnight they had become quite proficient at the "Mitre." Something had had to be done, and in one raid on our hostess's pantry *Tai-Mo-Shan* had been enriched to the tune of 72 jellies and 47 pots of jam !

I accompanied the doctor to Nikko, which is well worthy of a visit. It is some $2\frac{3}{4}$ hours by train from Tokio. On arrival there a motor was procured and took us up the mountains by a winding road to a height of some four thousand-odd feet. The salmon-trout from the lake made the most delicious eating. After being in China for three years, the air here was wonderfully exhilarating. The view is said to be one of the best in the world. As we arrived at night, after darkness had set in, we looked forward eagerly to viewing it at daylight. Next morning, chancing to wake up early, I was disappointed to find that a thick mist reduced the visibility to some ten yards. On awakening my companion, I was amused to find him at once looking out of the window, and then, without so much as a word, removing his monocle and polishing it vigorously on the bed-clothes.

A funicular railway takes one down to Nikko again, where there are numerous temples to be visited, lying in beautiful grounds. A lasting impression was made by a certain temple corridor with a red-lacquered floor which has the appearance of a mirror, due to the countless thousands of slippered feet which have shuffled along it.

Tokio is remarkable for the number of department-stores and the extremely low cost of the goods for sale. Mountaineering and camping kit was very prominent, and as we intended living ashore in the Aleutian Islands we provided ourselves here with the necessary equipment.

We had minor repairs done to our boat, such as the addition of a large ready-use fresh-water tank holding twenty-five gallons. This allowed for a longer period before pumping up more water from the tanks was necessary, and proved a useful addition to the boat. We also had our sails tanned a dark brown, which helps to preserve the canvas, which is apt to get rotten very quickly in damp tropical conditions.

We had two official parties at Yokohama, one given us by the Yacht Club and the other by the Master Mariners' Association. The first was a lunch-party, at which we were welcomed by the Commodore and members, and were the recipients of their club burgee. The second was an evening affair, and five beautiful Geisha girls attended to the wants of each of us during the meal. They certainly were most efficient at refilling the glasses of saké, so that this function became a rather less formal one than is normally the rule with official parties. Luckily we had become fairly experienced in the art of handling chopsticks during our time on the China Station.

Some of the Japanese young ladies are extremely dainty and attractive, and, as in other parts of the East, western fashions are making their influence felt both in the wearing of European clothes and in the dressing of the hair. In many cases the shorter hair of western fashion is preferred to the high erection common to Japanese ladies in the past. We certainly met some charming young ladies. One evening a young lady presented the one of us that she had chosen as her favourite with a little brown-paper parcel. She explained in her broken English that it contained five Japanese charms, and each of us was to hang one around his neck, to ensure protection from the gods. I am afraid that the other four could not quite see why they should comply with this request! This same little Japanese girl, who was extremely pretty, went to her temple one day and sought out the image of her favourite god, Buddhist or Taoist I know not. On her way to the temple she had purchased two hundred candles. She offered up one hundred of these, but promised the remainder when she had news of our safe arrival home. As a final act of devotion, she gave up drinking tea, which is a very favourite beverage in Japan, and she would only drink hot water instead. This sacrifice was also to last until our arrival home, so that one of the party at any rate felt quite miserable when some unavoidable delays made the voyage a slightly longer one than that originally anticipated.

There was another little girl who thought that our doctor's monocle was a decoration for valour.

We had one memorable dinner-party in Tokio with our naval friends. When we arrived at the restaurant, we removed our shoes and, donning slippers, we sat cross-legged on mats in a circle. In the centre sat a fine-looking Japanese man, and between him and us was a revolving table. He cooked the most excellent prawns with a specially delicious sauce, the recipe of which is said to be jealously guarded. He would carefully place a little pile of prawns in front of each guest in that half of the circle which he was facing at the moment. When he considered that they had enough to get on with, round he swung to face the other half of the circle. The shouts for him to turn round in the direction favourable to oneself turned the meal into rather an uproar.

We received the letter given below from someone whom we never had the pleasure of meeting, as he lived some three days' rail-journey away from Yokohama. As it was written in Japanese it occasioned us a little difficulty, until we were able to find somebody who could translate it for us.

" 21st June, 1933.
(Address)

Lieut.-Commander, Esq.

Sir,

It is owing to the report of to-day's paper, *The Tokyo Nichi-Nichi*, that I take the liberty of writing and of expressing to you the great admiration I have felt as to your fine undertaking that you have tried to sail to Pottsmas[1] from Hong-Kong, why so far distance of 15,000 miles in such a small yacht as only 22 tons.

[1] Portsmouth.

In the first place you have succeeded the voyage between Hong-Kong and Yokohama and arrived in Yokohama at 11.40 a.m. yesterday.

The paper reports that your boat has shown her light-green body waving the Union Jack and appearing on deck your brave and noble figure only having on simple white shirts and shorts off the coast of Yokohama.

What a boldness you have done, indeed !

What a pride of your Navy which had ever so famous Admiral Nelson. Great British will be crown of powers.

I hope you may rest enough to refresh and prepare all arrangement for next sailing while you are staying here for ten days given.

I hope you may succeed to return your home safely after finished the fine undertaking.

Good luck to our friend British and my dear and honourable you and attendants.

I am

Yours Truly,

Etc."

We decided that we did not want to make our stay at any one place of too long a duration, no matter how or by whom we might be tempted to prolong it. So on our twelfth day after arrival we got going again, bound for Hokkaido, the northernmost island of Japan. We laid in an additional stock of certain provisions, as we knew this would be our last opportunity of doing so before our arrival at Victoria, on the other side of the Pacific. As was our custom, we loaded up once more with as many fresh provisions as we could stow and a fresh supply of 500 eggs. These we simply greased, which keeps them fresh almost indefinitely. We still had some of our original supply from Hong-Kong, but as the salt in which they were packed was apt to penetrate through the pores, we found that some of the yolks were as hard as cannon-balls in consequence.

We embarked another passenger here, in the form of a monkey. He was on the end of a chain but, taking fright, promptly fell overboard in the harbour and had to be rescued. When we came to weigh our anchor we were unable to do so, as it had fouled some telephone-cables. However, this was rectified by swimming down to it, and with a final farewell to the little party of ladies who had come to bid us farewell, we left Yokohama under a large escort of steamboats, on the afternoon of Saturday the 1st July.

CHAPTER VI

Northern Waters

After leaving Yokohama we experienced day after day of drizzle and fog, and very often complete calms. At intervals the sun would break through and make a welcome change. After a week we had covered a distance of six hundred and forty miles—a daily average of 91½ miles. We were then just south of the north-east point of the island of Hokkaido. This left us with some forty miles to reach Nemuro, our next port of call. For two days we had been sighting various birds, and also whales and porpoises. We had sighted our first albatross by now, and also shot an Arctic skua. It was then so calm and the wind so light that by diving overboard we were able to retrieve the corpse.

The air temperature was 50° Fahrenheit at this time, and dropping fairly fast. In the early mornings there was a very distinct nip in the air, and in my diary for the 8th July I noted : " I gave them porridge, scrambled eggs (eleven) and bacon and beans. The coffee was quite good, too." For the previous evening meal I had apparently fixed them up with macaroni-cheese, with boiled cabbage, boiled parsnips and potato-balls, followed by plum pudding and coffee, and I add : " I am launching out quite a lot these days, and my victims are quite good about it. I do wish though that I understood how to work beef-suet. In making my first pudding

I got covered with the stuff, and so were all the cloths, buckets and kitchen utensils."

The fact of the matter was that it was a most tranquil existence, and we really had very little desire to reach anywhere. Two days before our arrival we were lying peacefully becalmed in the fog when along came a Japanese fishing-vessel. She came alongside and we got a fine salmon-trout and three other fish, which we were unable to identify. The former was dished up with lemons from Yokohama and tinned prawns, and was excellent. When we came to clean the other fish we discovered that they were full of worms, as was to be the case with such a great percentage of the fish that we later caught in the Pacific Ocean. Needless to say, we quite lost our appetite for them after our doctor had made this discovery, and we returned them from whence they came. I am afraid that the monkey did not do a very great portion of the trip with us. He looked so thoroughly miserable with the increasing cold and sea-sickness that we were glad that with our very complete medical stores we were able to ensure a perfectly painless death. I do not think that, apart from a cat, the keeping of pets under similar conditions is to be encouraged. This reminds one of Josh Slocum, the pioneer of lone sailors, who, having been presented with a goat, was dismayed to find that it had devoured his only chart of the West Indies, to which he was next proceeding.

During the final forty-eight hours we had thick fog and only light winds, conditions which were not conducive to sailing records. In twenty-four hours we had only made good twelve miles when the wind freshened slightly and gave us a speed of about three knots. We were working the lead continuously and we passed the lighthouse at the entrance to Nemuro harbour and anchored inside at four-thirty on the morning of the tenth of July. We had covered 680 miles in eight and a half days, giving a daily average of eighty miles.

Nemuro proved to be a snug little harbour which served a small fishing-town. The officials here spoke even less English than at our previous ports of call, but they examined our papers very conscientiously, and by use of a few simple words quite a hearty conversation was carried on. One unfortunate incident arose here. As soon as we had anchored, a Japanese gentleman arrived on board with a camera, and requested us to pose for a photograph. We complied with his wishes a little unwillingly. We had hoped that now we were getting into less civilised parts we would escape from that publicity which is demanded by the insatiable public appetite of the modern world. When the photograph had been taken, we explained in pidgin English that we wanted five copies of the photograph in return for having posed for it. In addition, one of us, feeling that the presence of the local photographer on board was a suitable opportunity for the development of his own photographs, produced a film. This he gave to him, and after gesticulating with his fingers he thought that he had made it quite clear that what he required was five prints of each. The photographer, promising to return later in the day, left us. True to his word, back he came that afternoon. He produced five copies of the group, and then, putting his hand into his robe, he handed our friend his photographs. These proved to be excellent ones, but there was only one print of each photograph instead of the five demanded. The poor man was greeted with such outbursts of " Five-piecy this one, savvy ?—Five-piecy this one, savvy ? "—until it was quite clear what was required. He was bundled unceremoniously over the side into his dinghy, and pulled out of range of earshot at high speed. He must have worked overtime, for quite shortly after-wards the required prints arrived. He demanded no money, and in fact shook his head vigorously when offered it. The following evening, two of the crew were strolling around the streets of the little town, when a Japanese gentleman stood in front of them. With his hands tucked into the wide sleeves of his silk gown, he bowed profusely. For a moment they were a little non-plussed, and then they recognised the photographer of the day before. " You come my house ? " he asked questioningly, with an intake of breath through his teeth, and once more he repeated this question, but more insistently the second time. Only too pleased to see more of the life in this quaint little town than strolling around its streets offered them, they readily assented.

They were surprised when, after removing their shoes, their host ushered them into a spacious house. They followed him across the matting and noted the few jade ornaments on little pedestals which, with a few delicate Japanese prints hanging on scrolls down the wall, gave to the room across which they were passing that artistic appearance which only the Japanese knows how to achieve in such a simple manner. They had to lower their heads as they passed through the opening into the next room. Mats were arranged on the ground around a low wooden table on which the presence of bowls, chopsticks and blue-patterned saké cups seemed to indicate that everything had been got ready for their entertainment. They complied with their host's invitation to be seated, and lowering themselves on to the mat in a rather less dignified manner than he did, they endeavoured to arrange themselves cross-legged as though they had done it all their lives. It was while their host was clapping his podgy hands together to summon the maidservant that they had their first opportunity of studying the room in which they were seated. There were the usual little ornaments and thin wooden walls, but what really did surprise them was to see standing in one corner a large glass-fronted cupboard. It had numerous shelves, on which were rows of medical instruments. The entrance of a dainty little girl interrupted their thoughts for a moment. She bowed low to each one of them in turn, and then turned to her master to receive his instructions. As she stood before him, a small child suspended in a silk band on her back regarded them curiously with its large round eyes, its chubby fingers clawing at her shoulders as if to ensure that there was no possibility of parting company from its protector.

When the swish-swish of her slippers had died away, our doctor, who was one of the party, was eager to satisfy his curiosity about the contents of the cupboard in the corner. Pointing to it, he asked the reason for its presence. Our host, though he understood little English, was noticeably keen to explain it to his guests, and took them over to examine it. The arrival of the leading citizens of the town again temporarily interrupted him. Introductions were made all round, and low bowing and handshakes completed the formalities. Among the new arrivals was an officer of the customs whose English was of a high standard, and it was to him that the doctor turned to seek light on the medical equipment. Imagine their surprise, therefore, when the two of them learned that their host was the leading doctor of the town and had a large practice. In mistaking him for the photographer, and plying him with photographic work to be done, they felt that they had made a grievous error. It was explained that he practised photography and had come on board on the arrival of the boat to indulge in his hobby. When the profuse apologies for the trouble to which they had put him had been re-translated by the customs officer, he beamed with delight on his guests. His excitement knew no bounds when he discovered that one of the Englishmen was a qualified doctor, and for some hours the interpreter was kept extremely busy.

The young Japanese lady kept bending over the shoulders of the assembled guests and refilling the little china cups with hot saké. The pleasant atmosphere of the gathering seemed to be reflected in the host's bearing, as he kept repeating, " This very pleasant, this very pleasant ! "

The three youngest members of the crew decided to stretch their legs one afternoon, to combat the lack of exercise on board ship. As soon as they landed they were joined by a member of the local police force. Since they were clad in suitable attire and had the advantage of the fitness of youth over their escort, they were soon outdistancing him. In order to keep up with them he had to run, and I feel that if he did not think westerners a little mad before this, he certainly does now. They found that the country here was flat and rather uninteresting ; it was little cultivated and only slightly populated.

The prospects of obtaining a haircut for some considerable time were very uncertain. After leaving Yokohama we had all grown beards. These were now of varying length, texture and colour. We found a barber's shop in Nemuro of good size. We had one member of the crew who was constantly taking a look at his beard in the glass, and who considered it far superior to the remainder. He had a haircut at the local hairdresser's, and when it was completed, the man who was doing the job for him proceeded to soap his apology for a beard, preparatory to shaving it off. The unfortunate barber, left standing with a soapy shaving-brush in his right hand, looked extremely surprised when his victim leaped out of the chair with a wild yell !

There were fresh vegetables to be obtained here, and we laid in as large a stock as the existing space would allow of. The police again came to our assistance and obviated the language difficulty by taking control of the money which I had been allowed for the purpose, and buying more for the value of it than I could possibly have succeeded in doing without their aid.

At noon on Thursday the 13th of July we sailed from Nemuro, despite foggy weather, as a fresh breeze was blowing from the north-east. Our object now was to sail up to the Aleutian Islands, which we had decided to visit before crossing the Northern Pacific Ocean. As a glance at the map will show, our latitude at this time was only a little north of San Francisco. The northern route taken by the Canadian Pacific Steamships from Yokohama to Vancouver passes south of the Aleutian Island group, but sufficiently close for the southernmost of them to be sighted on a clear day.

North of the island of Hokkaido, in which Nemuro is situated, is the Okhotsk Sea, and forming its south-eastern boundary are the Kurile Islands. These run in a north-easterly direction right up to the southernmost tip of Kamchatka, the heart-shaped appendage which, protruding from Siberia, forms the north-eastern boundary of this sea. We were bound to pass close to the southern islands of the Kurile group, but, unless we had to do so in case of emergency, we did not intend to break our journey there but to make one of the Aleutian Island group our next stop.

At this period of our voyage we had a great feeling of suppressed excitement. We had a sense of sailing in waters which were unstirred by the passing of giant liners and numerous steamships. To the west of us lay the Kurile Islands, away to the north the Aleutian group, and beyond them the Bering Sea, leading into the Arctic Ocean. When we had first talked over our trip we had discovered to our dismay that in these days of quick travel the very ends of the earth seem to have been reached. However, adventure can never be dead, and we were sailing through waters now where men of various nationalities had passed their lives in adventurous pursuits.

The Kurile Islands have been known to the Japanese

for some five centuries, but as far as European exploration was concerned it was not until the year 1634 that
they were discovered. For that year they were found
by a Dutchman named De Vries. Twenty years after
him, a Russian merchant named Taras Stadukin sailed
from Northern Siberia, through the Bering Strait,
along the coast of Kamchatka, and so found the northernmost islands of the group. As a result of his dis-
coveries, the northern islands were dominated by the
Russians, who soon levied a fur-tax on the Ainu inhabitants. It was found that these waters abounded
with sea-otters at that time. These animals were
extremely valuable on account of their fine pelts. To
deal with them the Russians introduced Aleuts, who
were far better otter-hunters than the unfortunate
Ainus. About sixty years ago the whole group was
handed over to Japan, and in 1884 all the remaining
natives, who numbered under one hundred, were
settled on the more southerly island of Shikotan. This
was the island that we were to sight on Saturday, the
fifteenth of July. Such delightful names as Frying-Pan
Bay, Clam Bay, are marked on old maps of this island.

All these islands are of volcanic origin, and are the
breeding-place of innumerable sea-birds, of which
fulmars, guillemots, little auks and puffins are but a few.
A cold Arctic current (the Oyashiwo), whose average
summer temperature is 35° F., sets along their shores
in a south-westerly direction, and further eastward,
running in the opposite direction, is the warm Japanese
current (the Kuroshiwo). The ice lasts around here
until May, and throughout the summer fog is almost
everlasting. The worst month of the year for this is

July. Currents and heavy tide-rips run around the shores, but thick fields of kelp give one a good warning of approach to the islands even in fog.

Of sea-animals there used to be numerous sea-otters, fur-seals, sea-lions, whales, blackfish, killers and porpoises. However, the first of these provided such adventurous hunting that now they are seldom to be found. The hunting of these sea-otters had been carried out by the Ainu natives, but in a primitive fashion. They shot at them from the rocks with bow-and-arrows, or in the winter clubbed them to death on the ice.

About 1870 foreigners started to arrive. I believe that the credit for initiative belongs to Captain Kimberley of the American schooner *Cygnet*. He was soon followed by British, Russians and Japanese, who were beginning to realise the money-making opportunities of these animals. In the nine years after a real start had been made on a large scale, over 10,000 pelts were taken. The method of securing these animals was by pursuing them in boats and shooting them as they came to the surface. By the time some sort of international control had been instituted, sea-otters had all but ceased to exist.

As we passed along the eastern shore of Shikotan our thoughts were occupied with the activities of the past in these very waters.

CHAPTER VII

Attu in the Aleutian Islands

At the end of one week's sailing under very light weather conditions we had covered 290 miles, leaving us some 1,200 miles yet to do before reaching Attu in the Aleutian Islands. We were then to the north-eastward of Yetorup Island. We began to think that it would take us another month to get to the Aleutian Islands. We were, however, getting quite used to the rather slow progress, and if it did mean delay it at least had the advantage of making life on board very comfortable. The fixing of the ship's position was not an easy matter, but our navigator was exceptionally successful at getting results whenever the weather cleared sufficiently to give him time to shoot the sun.

The temperature was round about 50° F., but varied very noticeably according to the proximity of the warm or cold current which I have mentioned in the previous chapter. The temperature off Attu was 43° F., but when in the warm current it rose to 55° F. We had seen a few cormorants and albatrosses. The two types of albatrosses seen were the black-footed and the laysan, while there were also many puffins. We were surprised to find that such short-winged birds strayed so far from land which was 100 miles away. We all felt fighting-fit and were enjoying the freshness of this northern atmosphere after three years in the Tropics. In fact, the only incident of note at this period to disturb our calm was when I had half my moustache burned off by the flaring-up of a stove. We decided to try out our harpoon gun, which was an old-fashioned affair. Everything was prepared and, as the largest, I was detailed to fire it, and stood trembling with it in my hands. When all was ready, there was some hesitation on my part, for I found that I was standing with the hatchway just behind me, and I had lost my nerve, fearing to be knocked backwards down into the galley. However, the harpoon left the gun most successfully, struck the water some seventy-five yards away, resumed its flight, and disappeared again some 100 yards off. The shackle to which it was joined was intact, so the head of the harpoon must have given way. Possibly we had used too strong a charge of powder, but as we had only a small supply of harpoons we decided to postpone further trials until we could carry them out in shallow water.

Our next adventure was a fire, the big dread of all yachtsmen. One of the pressure-stoves, which were in a leaky condition by this time, had flared up. It soon turned the compartment in which it was housed into a veritable furnace. Its removal, without very severe burns in consequence, was out of the question. There was only one thing to do, and that was to apply the fire-extinguisher. This was altogether effective, but the mess which it caused both in the galley and the surrounding compartments beggars description. While I was viewing it with dismay, a shout from the helmsman brought us all on deck.

C

It appeared that the afternoon watchman had been awakened from his day-dreams by a loud, hissing noise, and he declared that some enormous creature had disappeared from view close astern, before he could identify it. They—for there were two of them—turned out to be Rorqual whales. They certainly looked tremendous at such close range, and we were deeply interested when one of them passed under the boat. We did not relish the idea of having to return home at this stage and tell our friends that we had lost our boat by being capsized by a whale ! After the first eleven days, the wind showed signs of freshening, with a consequent increase in our daily run. Up to then our track on the chart in search of wind must have looked extremely odd. It is interesting to note that this was logged as Force 3 [1] (7-10 m.p.h.) on Monday, 3rd July, our third day out from Yokohama, and did not exceed Force 2 [1] (4-6 m.p.h.) until Saturday, 22nd July, when it again rose to Force 3.

On the following Monday and Tuesday our day's runs were 95 and 132 miles, which was a decided improvement. On Wednesday, from 7 a.m. to 4 p.m., the barometer had dropped from 29·94 to 29·70. The wind increased to gale force by nightfall and by midnight we had hove-to under reefed mizzen and staysail aback. Owing to our rather rapid departure from Hong-Kong we had not had the opportunity of trying the boat out under real rough-weather conditions, and so we were naturally interested to see how she would behave. The barometer dropped to 29·6, and the wind increased to about 70 m.p.h. The vessel lay quite com-

[1] Beaufort Scale.   See Appendix.

fortably about six points off the wind, and we remained hove-to until half-past six the following evening. We discovered later, through the kindness of the American Meteorological Officer at Dutch Harbour, who examined his records, that this was a typhoon which had passed up into the Bering Sea instead of curving away in an easterly direction over Japan, as is their usual custom.

When we continued on our course it was with renewed confidence in our craft, which had behaved so splendidly and of which we were already growing so extremely fond. The gale had cleared the atmosphere, which was so clear that on the evening of Sunday the 30th July we sighted the Aleutian Islands when seventy miles away. The following morning we were very disgusted when low visibility forced us to heave-to again. Luckily it only lasted for a short time, and by half-past twelve we were on our way once more. That afternoon no one slept. We were all on deck, watching the marvellous scenery. There was still plenty of snow on the hills, and huge silvery waterfalls cascaded down the steep cliffs into the ocean below.

It was a race against time. Should the wind hold, we could make an entrance into the little harbour of Attu before dark. Should we fail to do it in daylight, we knew we would have to wait till the following morning, and as this was our eighteenth day at sea, the prospects of lying peacefully at anchor that very evening seemed most attractive. At 6 p.m. this important entry appeared in the ship's log : " Commenced beating into Chicagof Harbour, Attu." By five minutes past seven we were at anchor. The total mileage from Nemuro to Attu was 1,354, which took us eighteen days, giving us a daily average of seventy-four miles.

When we rounded the eagerly-awaited point we caught our first glimpse of Attu. High hills covered with wild flowers, except where numerous valleys bore traces of their winter covering, for deep drifts of snow still remained, formed the background to a most attractive little bay. At the foot of the hills nestled a neat little row of houses, nine in all. Their white walls and red roofs made a picturesque sight. At one end, as if to balance the perfect model village, was the church with its square tower surmounted by a dome, while at the other end stood a recently-erected school-building.

As we tacked up the little bay on a perfect summer evening, flocks of puffins propelled their plump, stumpy bodies through the air at an incredible speed, while the evening sunshine was reflected on their coloured bills. The cause of their disturbance was soon evident to us. We saw a native boat coming towards us, and we were greatly surprised to find that she was fitted with an outboard engine. Several natives were in her, and, taking station ahead of us, motioned to us to follow. When they had led us to our anchorage they came alongside, but hesitated to come on board. We then noticed that they were shivering, and we were surprised to think that, though it was distinctly cold, the natives of the place should feel it. We were to learn later that they were afraid that we were some enemies of theirs who had come to steal their furs.

The information in the Pilotage Handbook for these waters had been pieced together from the visits of warships, but as none had visited there for many years, the information was somewhat out of date. It stated that a Russian trader was believed to live there and carry on a trade with the natives. We soon discovered that the natives spoke English, and they were eager to hear what was happening in Manchukuo when they discovered whence we had come. We in return eagerly interrogated them about the Russian trader, to which they replied that there was no Russian trader ashore, but there was an American named Fred. We assembled our little canvas boat and hurried ashore to make his acquaintance.

We soon found Fred, who of course knew nothing about us and was waiting on the beach to welcome us. His solitude must have been rudely disturbed by the arrival of five young British officers. However, as he seemed almost as glad to have us to talk to as we were to hear his stories, we took him back on board to supper.

There are no other villages on this island, which is the westernmost one of the group. When we arrived there were forty-nine inhabitants. The number was increased to fifty the following day. They said that the new arrival was going to be christened Tai-Mo-Shan. These islands belong to America. This one differed slightly from the remainder in that most of them are loaned to private individuals for the purpose of fox-breeding, but this one was loaned to the natives. The natives, Aleuts, live by trapping these foxes during the winter months.

This American, whom we will call Fred, for that is the name by which the natives of the place knew him, was expecting the arrival of a ship to transport him to San Francisco, and thought it might arrive any day in the near future. However, wrecks occur in that part of the world with great frequency. That evening, as the result of a good supper and, observing we were no longer at sea, some whisky, he regaled us with some of his experiences. We could have sat and listened to his adventures for hours on end. All were told in the most amusing way.

Fred had led an adventurous life. At one time he had worked in an hotel in Unalaska at the time of the gold-rush. This was a temporary job, for at a later period he was to spend exciting times in sea-otter and fur-seal-hunting, and also whaling in the Arctic Ocean and Bering Sea. I still remember some of the best of his stories ; how three schooners which he owned went " on the bum " at the same time ; how, on another occasion, he was both engineer and cook of a vessel which gave him little time for resting. He overcame this difficulty by lying in his bunk and manipulating the frying-pan with one hand and regulating the speed of the engines with the other. On another occasion his ship caught fire, and getting out of control they had to take to the boats. On this occasion he did 450 miles in the open boat.

At Attu he was keeping a store from which he sold goods to the natives. In return they trap the foxes and he buys the furs from them. The actual trapping takes place in December and January. There are other islands also under his control, for they can only trap each island in alternate winters. As Attu had been trapped the previous winter, all except one man were waiting to leave as soon as the ship arrived to fetch them, and they would then be landed on the next islands to be trapped. Though, as I have mentioned, the trapping takes place in the winter, the steamer only made two visits a year, one in April, when Fred arrived from San Francisco, and again about this time to take him back. In consequence, the natives had to take advantage of its arrival and await its return the following spring to collect them from the various islands. Fred had a partner with whom he sometimes managed to connect on his way south after trading with the Eskimos around Cape Barrow in the Arctic.

In the harbour they had " runs " of salmon, though that season had not been up to the average. They get the Sock-eye, the Silver and the Humpback salmon, in that order. There were a few of the first-named in the harbour when we were there, and it was a simple matter for the natives to net them. They were excellent eating, and as soon as we required a fresh supply we " traded " a torch-battery for each one brought on board.

The natives, though they are not related to them, were very like Eskimos in appearance. Apart from the trapping season, which lasts about two months, they do nothing all day. They were extremely friendly. The wood both for their houses and fires, etc. is collected from the beaches, on to which it drifts in a mysterious manner. There are no trees within two thousand miles, and yet though they get large timbers, this driftwood is seldom met with at sea. Presumably their arrival there must be the result of some under-running current. We found that they were absolutely dependent on Fred, who supplied them with tinned foods on account, the amount owing being squared with the settlement for the furs. One of their chief foods was salmon, and we were somewhat surprised to find that they preferred purchasing the tinned variety from the store, though there were always numbers to be had for the asking in the harbour. They had no other food of their own, but when asked why they did not cultivate some potatoes, etc., which would, I think, be perfectly suited by the climate, they said that they were too busy.

They elect their own chief, whom they hold in great respect. It was a man named Mike when we were there. He was an excellent native, and besides administering to their daily wants, looked after their spiritual ones in addition. He took us into the church, where he proudly displayed the signature of the distinguished German aviator, Von Gronau, who had called there some years previously when a world-flight was an even more hazardous undertaking than it is to-day. They had also benefited by the flight of a British aviator for whom quantities of food, cigarettes and petrol had been forwarded in advance. As, however, he had never reached there, they much appreciated his proposed visit. They were now delighted to renew their acquaintance with Gold Flake cigarettes.

When we were in the church we also noticed that the Bible was written in Greek, and were amazed to find that Mike had learned this language in Alaska some years previously. They were of the Greek Orthodox faith. Burials were accompanied by a great deal of singing, and though they constructed the coffin they relied on Fred for all repairs to their boats and houses. A short time before this, an American Government Department had called for the construction of a school there, and provided ample money for it. Fred, being on the spot, had obtained the contract and had completed it the previous year. It had sizeable classrooms, desks, stoves, and even a drug-store. There was no school-teacher on the island, and only five children of school age, so it had only once been used, and that was for a dance in which the villagers indulged. Next day all the wives had to scrub it out, and its doors were closed once more.

The natives were extraordinarily healthy, and among them were a few very old ones, though they were unable to tell us their ages. Our doctor got busy extracting some teeth. The first patient was a woman, who bore it extremely well. Indeed, she seemed to enjoy it so much that soon more would-be patients were demanding treatment.

We had a very restful stay here and, despite the cold, one party went off for three days' walking and camping inland, while the remainder soon began to feel the benefits of walks up the mountains.

One day we accompanied a native in his boat a short distance outside the harbour entrance. We then stopped the engine and lowered "jigs" over the side. These "jigs" consisted of a line, a weight, and three hooks. The fish that we were after were a type of herring peculiar to these waters, and could be seen swimming about in large shoals. No bait was used, and yet we caught sixty fish in half-an-hour, using only two lines. I would never have believed that fish could be so easy to catch. We took care to take a photograph when we hooked three at once ! When we were bored with this, we pushed out into deeper water and fished on the bottom. This time we had some mackerel as bait on one of the lines, but it did not seem any more successful than the line with just the bare hooks. We got cod in large quantities and we weighed four of these on our return. They totalled eighty-three pounds. On our way back the Aleut at the helm bumped over some rocks which were just below the surface. It was amusing to hear him remark: " Me bum captain."

There were flocks of sea-birds here, guillemots, auks, and puffins, or sea-parrots, as they call them. We had recently read a book about these parts by a sea-otter hunter. He had mentioned how, when he had been shipwrecked on the island of Yezo in the Kurile Islands, he had enjoyed excellent puffin stews. We decided to give them a trial. I was a little suspicious of their attractive eating qualities, for I had once been rash enough to supplement my midshipman's fare with a cormorant which, during the War, I had shot at Scapa Flow. On that occasion, which, as far as I was concerned, was a memorable one, owing to the unpopularity I had achieved by my action, the gun-room and its vicinity had smelt very powerful for some days. Now I got no option in the matter, for I was presented with half-a-dozen corpses which the remainder had shot. Try as I would, all tricks of the trade known to cooks were of little avail, and though they had been dipped in warm water, it was impossible to pluck them. Then it was that an amused Aleut stepped in and showed me their method of cutting around the neck and turning the feathers inside-out. They made the most excellent stew and were not in the least fishy, having a taste resembling calf's liver. On one day our fare was not so successful ;

we had a number of herring, and I must own that I had kept some of them over-long. I thought that if they were hung over the side their keeping propensities would be increased. However, such was evidently not the case, and our doctor had to come to our rescue as well as his own.

We watered the boat from a mountain stream, ferrying it off in barrels which we had borrowed from Fred for the purpose. We were running rather short of certain provisions, and as Fred was daily expecting the ship on which he and the natives were to leave, he gave us a quantity of eggs, etc. We felt very guilty afterwards, when we heard that sure enough his ship had been wrecked on its way up from San Francisco, and it was a long, weary wait of several weeks that he had there.

One native, who with age had learned wisdom, slipped on board just as we were leaving, and asked us to take his mail for Alaska, as he reckoned that we would get there before the steamer. So on Thursday, 10th August, carrying our first mail, we left this delightful little harbour.

CHAPTER VIII

Across the Bering Sea

Though we had made out a programme in the first place, we sometimes found it necessary to alter it according to existing circumstances. Such was the case on the next leg of our voyage. We had planned to spend some weeks in these out-of-the-way islands. On our voyage from Nemuro to Attu we had experienced a great deal of fog. The weather maps for that part of the Pacific put the percentage for the number of days of fog at that time of the year as high as sixty per cent. We experienced an even greater amount. The only thing to be remarked in its favour was the fact that it was usually accompanied by some wind, which is certainly not always the case in the waters around our own coasts. While we were at Attu the wind blew hard from one direction or another throughout our entire stay. Even though we were in harbour it was most useful, for we had a windmill generator as an alternative method of charging our batteries. This was a simple device and the windmill had its own fitting on the breakwater, where it was in nobody's way. However, as fog and strong winds alternate in these parts, Fred had strongly advised us not to sail in the vicinity of these islands. Heavy tide rips and uncharted rocks in their neighbourhood did not encourage us to disregard his advice. As we had no engine with which to combat these dangers we would have been extremely foolish to have done so.

The Bishop for these parts, who lives at Dutch Harbour, had recently been to see his flock. He was about seventy. The ship in which he was visiting the islands was unfortunately wrecked on one of them. Thirteen days later he was found. He was the sole survivor from the ship, and, despite his age and the intense cold, he had managed to keep alive by grabbing oranges as they were washed ashore from the wreck.

When we left Attu it was blowing a gale and our progress was greatly improved in consequence. We sailed up well to the north'ard into the Bering Sea, and our crossing of this sea was subsequently made at a distance of about 100 miles north of the islands. For the first three days the seas were so rough that both the interior of the boat and of ourselves suffered accordingly. Ryder was one of those amazing and fortunate people who remain quite unmoved, however violent the motion, and the more lively the latter became the keener he seemed to grow for his meals. The remainder of us were suffering from this distressing malady in varying degrees, but it only affected us for the first twenty-four hours after leaving harbour. After this, the renewed appetites called for increased work from the commissariat department. Once we had reached the recovery stage, no seas, however rough, affected us. On the other hand, windward work in a heavy sea gives a quick, bumpy motion. After a few days of this the interior of the vessel would lose all semblance of tidiness. In the galley paraffin and cooking-fat mixed with spray, which sometimes found its way down the hatch during the relieving of the watch, turning the sloping wooden deck into a veritable skating-rink. When we were on the port tack and the cook suddenly found himself sliding away from his stove, he had to be lashed with a canvas band. This left him with both hands free to prepare the food. Shortly after leaving Attu, one of the stoves gave trouble, and flared up so violently that a fire extinguisher had again to be brought into use. On another occasion a tin of Quaker Oats bounced off the table and emptied its contents on the deck. The porridge which it formed was of the highest order, but was very difficult to negotiate in rubber sea-boots !

Our meals were taken in the saloon, four of us feeding together while the other one looked after the steering of the boat. We found that both washing-up and the actual consumption of the food was more easily managed from bowls. We had some of the china variety, but these did not last long, and finally enamel ones were found to suit our purpose admirably. Owing to the angle at which we sometimes found ourselves, we had to adopt strange postures to prevent the contents of our bowls from mingling with the already greasy mixture which covered the deck. Fred had constructed a new arrangement of " fiddles," the name by which the wooden compartments for the table are known, which was most efficient, and enabled us to have a good supply of necessaries easily at hand.

After a few days of good sailing the visibility was again blotted out by fog. It was more unwelcome than ever just then, for we were contemplating visiting a most interesting island. This island, which is known as Bogisloff, is like the remainder of the islands around these parts in that it is of volcanic origin. In fact, new portions of it appear from time to time, while other parts of it disappear. The consequence is that its position is never too certain, and the American coastguard ships have to check this afresh when they visit these parts. At that time of the year it is the home of countless seals, who make landing on it by boat a most exciting event. We were therefore full of regrets when the foggy weather continued, and we had to give Bogisloff a wide berth. Not many people have business in these parts, but on one occasion the captain of a steamer which visited there noted the extraordinary number of sea-birds which shared the island with the seals for breeding purposes. On a subsequent visit to the island he was surprised to find that the latter were in sole possession. Further examination revealed the corpses of hundreds of these sea-birds, who had evidently been caught unawares by a disturbance of volcanic origin.

At the time that we were sailing in these northern latitudes a scientific expedition was visiting the islands. They were under the direction of an American priest named Father Hubbard, and were engaged in excavation work at the site of prehistoric villages. A subsequent account was published of their visit to Bogisloff and the great difficulty that they had in preventing their boat from being swamped by the onrush of seals which greeted them.

We had been unable to check our position since leaving Attu, and though we were making good progress we were growing increasingly anxious to ensure that adverse currents were not setting us inshore. We did not therefore relish the idea of closing the shores of Unalaska without first verifying our position in regard to them. Modern invention was to come to our aid. Our wireless-operator had been quite busy, and had sent a signal on short-wave intended for the Amateurs of Hong-Kong, which, we later heard, was received there. As this was close on 3,000 miles direct, it was a cause of satisfaction when we heard of it. Francis, our " Sparker," as telegraphist ratings are familiarly termed in the navy, decided to try his luck at getting a bearing of the wireless station at Dutch Harbour, for which we were bound. He constructed a small frame aerial and suspended it from a suitable hook in the beams above his head. Meanwhile, a small hand-bearing compass was held alongside, and when the frame aerial denoted the correct bearing we read it off. It was the simplest arrangement and we did not expect our results to prove very accurate. However, we acted on his findings, steering the course which should take us to the entrance of the harbour. We could still see nothing, as a combination of lo, clouds and fog prevented us from doing so. Our confidence in his predictions was not misplaced, for his bearing proved correct to within three degrees. We found that we had been set well to the northward during our passage along the Bering Sea.

This sea is only free of ice for a few months of the year. We had chosen about the best possible time to make our crossing of it, and though it was extremely cold we did not sight any ice. Our only visitors were baby fur-seals who had doubtless seen the light of day for the first time on Bogisloff Island. We were quite close to that island when a glossy black head popped out of the water, soon to be followed by another. They were not taking risks, however, with this foreign intruder, and their rapid evolutions would have made them an extremely difficult target. We did not contemplate any such treacherous actions, and so they became very bold. They would come very close and have a good look, and while doing so their little heads were stuck out above the surface so rigidly as to give one the impression that they must be resting their tails on the bottom of the ocean. A thin line of sparkling bubbles showed their swimming capabilities as they darted around us, their tracks curving and crossing as they gave vent to their obvious enjoyment.

The weather cleared as we approached the land, and our first view of it impressed us as much as the first sighting of the Aleutian Islands had done a short time previously. A curtain of white clouds hung around the steep cliffs, and again great waterfalls poured from their summit into the sea. A most favourable breeze added to our enjoyment as we made a swift progress towards the narrow harbour-mouth.

There were really two separate harbours, and as we passed the entrance to the first we could see a row of houses bordering the shore. We sailed into Illiuliuk Harbour, the inner arm of Dutch Harbour. As we rounded the buoy close to the shore we could see some cameras recording our entrance. It was amusing to us, for we had taken a rather wider sweep around it than we should have done, and the channel being narrow we actually found ourselves on the soft mud. We slid off again a minute or two later, and I don't suppose that the cameras recorded this ignominious incident.

A motor-boat came along and offered us a tow. Aboard was Mr. Pedler, the genial representative of the Alaska Commercial Company, who have extensive interests in these parts. We were glad to accept it as, owing to the head-wind, we would otherwise have been some time in tacking up the narrow channel. As we approached the wharf we saw an American coastguard-cutter, whose ship's company were regarding us with interest. They had some sailors on the arm of the jetty to secure us. We were keen to carry out a seamanlike evolution in view of the presence of the American sea-men, whom we were meeting for the first time in our voyage. We stationed ourselves at various positions on deck with heaving lines. The stem approached the jetty. The bowman swung the coil of rope in his right hand and with the impetus thus achieved gauged his moment, and sent it hurtling towards the sailors above him. Unfortunately he was so pleased with the fulfil-ment of his plans that he let go the remainder of the coil of line, which also followed suit before he could retrieve the inboard end. This was the first amusing incident of a very happy stay which we were to enjoy as the guests of the officers of the American Coastguard Service. Our arrival there added another 757 miles to our total. We had taken six days, and so our daily average for this leg came to 118.

CHAPTER IX

Dutch Harbour, Unalaska

Owing to the amount of space occupied by food-cupboards for the large quantity of food required on this trip, our washing arrangements were not extensive and, to be honest, were mainly confined to the upper deck. In cold weather, therefore, no very great importance was attached to this action. Indeed, were one to indulge in it one ran the risk of incurring the wrath of the doctor, who safeguarded the fresh-water supply. While salt-water soap was available, it was not found to be a very satisfactory substitute. In consequence, as one approached harbour, one's thoughts turned to endless hot water and a lather of soap.

Our American friends promptly sensed our require-ments, and for this purpose we at once repaired on board the coastguard-cutter *Tahoe*. She was lying at the same jetty as that at which we had just berthed. We were most refreshed by our baths and then proceeded to meet Commander Towle and his officers. We were disappointed to learn that they were going to sea the following day, but their place was taken by another coastguard-cutter, the *Chelan*, who also placed their ship at our disposal. I think that very little is known of the wonderful work done by these coastguard-cutters. A very great deal of their time was occupied in the hectic days of prohibition in the suppression of rum-

running. The latter, as you may know, existed on a
scale which would sound like a fairy-tale to the average
person in England, where the exciting days of extensive
smuggling are, perhaps unfortunately, a thing of the
past. But it was not only with the rum racket that they
were concerned. As I previously have mentioned, it is
only for a few months in the year that the Bering Sea
is clear of ice. During this time numbers of fishing-
vessels are active in those waters. These cutters are in
constant attendance on them, for in waters where tide
rips and powerful currents abound they often require
their assistance. They also supply medical aid both to
these vessels and to the natives of the islands. In consequence, it is their duty to be putting to sea when
weather conditions are forcing other vessels to seek
refuge in harbour. The captains of both these vessels
had been engaged on escort work from Gibraltar during
the World War.

An American naval ship, the *Argonne*, came in one
evening to refuel on her way down to San Francisco.
She had a bunch of aviators and their planes on board,
as they had been carrying out an aerial survey of the
Aleutian Islands. Their task had been no easy matter
in an area where fog is so prevalent. They promptly
sent a boat over to *Tai-Mo-Shan*, and the five of us had
dinner on board. We returned later to our own vessel,
taking some of their officers with us, and having reached
American soil for the first time, it was with a great
feeling of pride that we showed them our craft. It was
not long before we were discovering many mutual
friends in the Asiatic Fleet with whom we were so often
in company in China. Indeed, I would class Manila,

which we frequently visited, as one of the most hospitable ports in the whole world.

The small town which existed was inhabited by Aleuts, while a few Americans had their interests here. The natives were not so simple and unsophisticated as our friends on Attu Island, where outside influence has scarcely been felt. There was a large store, where walrus-tusks, bear and wolf skins from around Cape Barrow, right away north in the Arctic Ocean, joined company with fountain-pens and razors, the product of modern machinery. A few smaller stores, some wooden dwelling-houses and the native village completed the settlement. The other sides of the harbour were bordered by high hills covered with thick, springy turf and beds of rushes. As on the hills which surrounded Attu, so here also wild flowers grew in great profusion, and with the keen air made walking a most enjoyable pastime. During one of these walks, I was striding along with great energy when some movement attracted my attention. It was a sunny morning, with a beautiful clear atmosphere, and the lapping of the waves on the beach was the only sound to disturb the restful peace of my surroundings. I stopped to see what it was that had instinctively caused the sharpening of my senses. Then I saw them. Three little brown heads peered at me round a boulder. I returned their gaze without blinking an eyelid. They took courage and jumped on the rock, where they gambolled merrily in the sunshine. They were like squirrels, and I knew them to be " lemmings," of whose existence I had often read in books of northern parts. I strolled on through the thick turf and came to the slope of a hill, where some tombstones caused me to stop once more. It is seldom nowadays that a British warship visits the coast north of Victoria in British Columbia, though one was to do so about a year after our own visit. So I was interested to find some English graves here which had all been well looked after by the Americans, though the masses of wild flowers did away with the necessity for those artificial abominations which abound in more fashionable resting-places. Among the inscriptions was one to an able seaman from H.M.S. *Satellite*, dated 1896.

Everything at Dutch Harbour was very expensive, which is natural, observing that all food supplies and other necessities have to be shipped up here from America. The main industry carried on there is herring-salting. It also serves as a terminus for ships on their way up into the Arctic. When the ice allows they proceed up to the Cape Barrow region, where such articles as furs and walrus-tusks, which the Eskimos bring to them, are purchased in exchange for the more artificial goods required by the latter.

Unfortunately, at the time of our visit to Dutch Harbour no coastguard-cutter was going to the Pribiloff Islands. Now, as a glance at the map will show you, these islands lie in the Bering Sea. They are the breeding-place of countless thousands of fur-seals which are protected by the American Government, from whom it would have been necessary to obtain permission to make a visit. The seals come up from the western seaboard of America annually to form these extensive " rookeries." Following Pribiloff's discovery of the rookeries on these islands in 1786, the hunting of these fur-seals was pursued with unabated energy. It was a matter of time before their extermination was complete in the same way as had occurred with the ruthless slaughter of sea-otters. They were pursued in skin-boats and all sorts of odd craft, and meanwhile scared into long lines of slaughter by the clapping of boards and bones and waving of flags, while even the opening and shutting of umbrellas was considered a fair means of adding to their terror. The old prints of these activities form an amusing admission of the primitive methods employed. Now that protection is ensured to these animals, they may breed in peace, and the number of skins can be regulated. In return for their agreement to leave the seals unmolested, a share of the profits is paid by the American Government to the other Governments concerned.

The executive officer of one of these coastguard-cutters was a keen fisherman, and we accompanied him one day to the mouth of a river in the vicinity. The wild mountain scenery put one in mind of the more beautiful parts of Scotland. We fished for sea-trout, of which we caught large numbers, using imitation salmon-eggs as bait. The largest of these fish was twenty-four inches in length. The salmon in this river were so numerous that as one waded up-stream one had to kick them out of the way. They were of the hump-backed variety and were in the last stages of decay. Their one remaining ambition was to get up-stream to a convenient spot where they could lay their eggs, and die. As one discovered the ease with which one could catch the trout one wondered how small a percentage of the salmon-eggs on which they feed must survive. And yet for past centuries these fish have left the place of their birth for the sea, and after a given period have returned to it once more, to lay their eggs and fade away in favour of a new generation. There were plenty of teal and duck, but the latter are said to be very fishy, or so we concluded from the remark of an American sailor who was with us. When we were asking about the duck-shooting, or " hunting," as our American friends prefer to term it, he summed up the situation by saying, " Say, guess you eat two courses in one if you try them ! " A useful tip, possibly, in these days of hustle !

We were shown great hospitality in Dutch Harbour, and the time passed all too quickly. One morning we were asked to breakfast with the Marshal. Dan Ross was a fine-looking man of middle-age. He was the living image of the Marshal as depicted in those early cowboy films where men rode at break-neck speed and drew their pistols at the least provocation. We sat down to the largest dishes of eggs, bacon and hot cakes that I have ever seen set before one at a meal. His buxom wife provided us with an everlasting stream of fresh supplies, while our host boomed forth in a voice of thunder, " I knew what real hunger was when, in my youth, I was panning gold in Alaska, and I like to see hearty appetites." He certainly did not do so badly himself. It so happened that on the previous day we had all gone out, after breakfast, into the wilds for the day, and through an error we had missed our next meal, which was to have been in the evening. In consequence, we were able to do full justice to the ample fare which he and his wife had provided. Despite his encouraging words, however, he showed signs of obvious alarm when the pace failed to slacken after a considerable inroad must have been made into the available supply of hens' eggs at Dutch Harbour. In desperation, he joined his wife in the kitchen, and their joint activities brought us to a standstill.

We had cause to be very grateful to a certain lady who took our cook in hand when he admitted to being uncertain of how to make doughnuts. An appointment was promptly made for the following morning, at the request of the remainder. I expect that a certain house in Dutch Harbour will remember a rather embarrassed naval officer, with an apron covering his submarine sweater, who was instructed in the art of making doughnuts under somewhat more hygienic conditions than those to which he was accustomed. He was also supplied with a bucket of Alaskan sour-dough which, with the daily addition of a little flour, was to prove as useful to us as it did to those adventurous spirits of Alaska in the years gone by.

The final hospitality that we enjoyed was over in the neighbouring bay. This bay was bordered by a long row of wooden buildings which were entirely deserted. They stood as silent evidence to the brisk trade that had sprung up here during the gold-rush of '98. Most of them were of the saloon variety. It was while dining here with the Aeriologist, or Meteorologist, as it is more commonly termed in England, that we were able to study the track of the typhoon which had passed over us between Hokkaido and Attu. We enjoyed our first " roast " of many months, which our host had procured from the *Argonne* before her departure for San Francisco.

The month of August was now well advanced, and despite the attractions of these northern waters, we decided to set sail once more. On Wednesday, the 23rd August, the motor-boat of the Alaska Commercial Company again came to our aid, and with a fine send-off from the coastguard-cutter *Chelan*, and our several friends ashore, we set off on our southerly trip down the western coast of Canada.

CHAPTER X

We Reach Victoria, B.C.

The motor-boat which towed us clear of the harbour turned back as we hoisted our sails and passed out of the narrow entrance through which we had arrived six days before. We were full of optimism as to the good start that we would make, as a fresh breeze augured well. We were just clear of the entrance, but had not lost sight of the houses ashore, when the wind dropped completely. It was most aggravating, for we felt that we might have spent yet another day in those hospitable surroundings. Evening came, and we had not advanced more than a quarter of a mile throughout the day. On the following day, 24th August, this brief announcement in my diary describes the situation in a few words : " Spent to-day becalmed in Unalaska Bay ; we are regretting having left harbour." For several days afterwards we had nothing but light winds alternating with periods of complete calm.

When we just got sufficient wind we made for Akutan Pass, to take us out of the Bering Sea and into the Pacific Ocean once more. Here again we were thwarted by light winds. Heavy tides are always experienced in these passes, and in the past it has been the custom of sailing-ships, on the termination of their business in northern waters, to solicit the aid of a tug to ensure their safe passage through them. Now we had no option but to change our tactics. We therefore made for Unimak Pass and successfully negotiated it three days after our departure from Dutch Harbour.

It would take a much abler pen than mine to do full justice to the beauty of the scenery, but, even as I write now, some ten months later, I have an indelible impression of it painted on my mind. Saturday, 26th August, was ushered in with a fine golden sunrise which was reflected over a clear sky ; the sea was in the serenest of moods. Glistening in the rays of the early morning sun, Shishaldin volcano reared its pointed cone, which was covered with snow the gleaming whiteness of which completed the most perfect view I have ever enjoyed. Even the glory of Mount Fujiyama, which we had enjoyed while in Japan, was not more devastating in its beauty. Dotted about the horizon were smaller mountain peaks, seemingly ashamed to assert themselves in the presence of their bigger brother, who claimed such a lion's share of the beautiful panorama. A white ball of smoke balanced on the summit of the cone, as if loath to be parted from it. All day we watched the kaleidoscopic effect which alternating sunlight or clouds produced upon the scene.

During these calms we had not got the sea to ourselves, for astern of us was a most friendly gathering. At times there were a dozen or more sea-birds, consisting of both the black-footed and laysan albatrosses and several fulmar petrels. The latter looked like fat woodpigeons who had mistaken their element. We tried them with samples of various foodstuffs, but they did not appreciate our efforts until we had a fresh idea. One of our stocks of food which was not at all popular, and of which we had in consequence a large surplus, was a certain brand of herrings-in-tomato. We decided that this was a good opportunity to rid ourselves of some of·them. We emptied the first tin over the stern. There was an immediate commotion as several albatross swooped down upon the food. We were delighted with our success, as the first-comer proceeded to get its huge beak into action. Our joy was but short-lived. Promptly emptying the contents of its beak into the water once more the bird washed it in the sea, with a vigorous shaking of his head as if to ensure no single particle should remain. We had ample time to make a close study of these birds, which were so often to be our companions in the future. Their expressions, due to the shading around the eyc, are of a rather comical but friendly sort, and are set off by a beak which in size seems out of proportion to the rest of the bird. On these calm days it was fascinating to watch them first drifting astern and then catching us up once more. They would alight close at hand, with their great wings outspread and their feet stretched out in front of them. These striking the surface of the water beat a patter like falling rain, and would finally bring them to rest, when they would slowly fold their wings into position on their backs. The commotion caused by their arrival would die down, and once more they would drift close under our stern.

Shortly after passing into the Pacific from Unimak Pass, we got some successful broadcast music. We were a little surprised at first to hear " Who's Afraid of the Big Bad Wolf ? " booming forth into our little saloon. We were to hear this a great many more time before we had finished with the Pacific. The first station that we received was the one at Oakland, San Francisco.

September was ushered in very badly as far as one of us was concerned. The aching of a tooth was the cause of the trouble, and people with toothache are not suitable companions to have around in a small boat in the middle of the ocean. It was therefore readily agreed that he must lose it for good and all. The victim waited around rather dubiously while the doctor gave the stove its customary slanging as he pumped it into a roar. The saucepan was filled with water, and then there followed the tinkle of forceps, lances, " pincers," or whatever they term the extracting implements. Perhaps you have gathered by now that the writer was by no means a disinterested party to these activities ! Some of those little pink pills, the same shade as blotting-paper, which all visitors to the dental chair must have met, were then dropped into a glass of water, where they circled around on the bottom, discharging a mass of bubbles to the surface. There was no getting out of it. The surgery was arranged on the top stair of the ladder leading to the upper-deck from the galley, so the patient was able to sniff the ozone to renew his courage. Ryder stood by with the utensils and received orders to hold the patient steady ; the heavy swell caused both the doctor and patient to lurch badly at intervals. Francis at the helm put the bow up into the wind when he saw an extra large one approaching. All was ready.

Luckily the extraction was with " novocaine," and while this was being inserted around the tooth, Salt, the other half of the starboard watch, arrived with a camera. " What shall I set it to ?   One metre ? " he queried.   Had I not been held down so effectively I would have then reduced the crew to four.   The extraction was also photographed, and though the victim can at normal times lay no claim to good looks, he certainly did not appear at his best under these very trying conditions.   However, in all fairness to the excellent profession to which our doctor belongs, I hasten to add that this extraction was a most successful one.   All the same, I think that the other members of this august body would have been a little surprised could they have seen his beard which, as he bent over his patient, partly concealed his Chinese mandarin's coat whose inner lining, so he used to proudly inform us, was of new-born lamb.   Dentistry was therefore accomplished under more colourful surroundings than usual, though the suggestion that when the false tooth was inserted it should be fitted with a swivel at its base to cause it to " feather," went unheeded.

By the 2nd of September, which was one week out from Dutch Harbour, we had only accomplished 264 miles, giving the low daily average of thirty-eight miles.   Conditions rapidly improved, as hoped for, and in the following five days we covered 825 miles, giving the somewhat higher daily average of 165 miles.   By 8th September we were sighting the high land of Vancouver Island at intervals through the fog, which had appeared again.   We were very irritated at the way in which our fine run had been brought to a sudden end by this light weather.   We spoke our first steamer on that date, but she was unable to read our lamp, or else had no means of answering us. We carried a naval Aldis lamp, which was very powerful. By noon on the 8th we were noting in our diaries that we were expecting to be in harbour in twenty-four hours' time. We had one hundred and thirty more miles to do. We worked hard in the boat, and it looked cleaner than it had done for a very long period. We also shaved off our beards and began to assume a comparatively respectable appearance. This was our seventeenth day at sea, which probably accounts for the fact that on this day my diary records that one member of the crew had been forbidden to sing, though he was permitted to recite if he so desired !

That final distance, which in a good breeze would have been easy of accomplishment in twenty-four hours, took some doing. Our patience was stretched to its limit. For four days we were becalmed in the vicinity of the lightship off the entrance to the channel leading up to Victoria and Vancouver beyond. We had thick fog and moved backwards and forwards on the tides, and by the end of that period we knew the appearance of the *Swiftsure* lightship perfectly.

On Monday, 11th September, we crawled up the Juan de Fuca Straits towards the Race Rocks in the evening. There was still thick fog, but a light following breeze helped us along. A large liner coming down-channel passed us some 200 yards distant, and shortly afterwards we heard the fog-signals of another steamer approaching from astern. Then followed a most hair-raising half-an-hour. We were making the prescribed fog-signal of three blasts for a sailing-ship with the wind astern. We used for this purpose an antiquated fog-horn which resembled a pair of fire-bellows. Our signal seemed to convey some other meaning to this ship, which altered course all over the place as soon as she arrived in our vicinity. She would then sound three blasts on her syren and rapidly disappear astern. As we would not see her lights until she was almost on top of us, owing to the fog, we were most relieved when she eventually passed us. Though we illuminated our sails with the signalling-lamp, it is doubtful whether the captain of this ship could see us. Presumably he mistook our signal for a motor fishing-vessel going astern. Of course, sailing-ships are comparatively rare these days.

By noon on Tuesday the 12th we were within a yard or two of the entrance to Victoria Harbour. The wind completely disappeared, and though we could nearly have jumped ashore, we had no hope of negotiating the entrance. A motor-boat came to our aid, and by half-past twelve we were moored in front of the imposing Empress Hotel. We had done 1,732 miles in twenty days—a daily average of eighty-six miles.

CHAPTER XI

We Arrive in the U.S.A.

We were not long in Victoria Harbour before our arrival became known to the officers of the Royal Canadian Navy. We were again shown remarkable hospitality and a launch was sent to tow *Tai-Mo-Shan* around to the neighbouring harbour of Esquimalt. She was moored alongside the jetty at Esquimalt Naval Barracks, and we were accommodated in the officers' quarters.

Victoria and Esquimalt form a favourite anchorage for many retired naval officers, so we were to enjoy a very full programme of social activities while here. We also wished to clean the bottom of our boat. Luckily there was a large slipway, belonging to Yarrow, a son of the famous old British shipbuilder. He insisted on having us put up on his slip, whence he had the accumulations of several months removed. She was, as a matter of fact, remarkably clean. A brand-new coat of paint made her look splendid.

One morning a stranger poked his head down the hatchway, and on being interrogated as to his wants, replied that he wished for a passage back to the " old country." He added that he would join on as cook. However, it was to the cook of *Tai-Mo-Shan* that he was addressing his remarks, so that the latter was able to express both his regret at being unable to oblige him and the great esteem in which the present cook was held. We also received a cable from an English Sunday newspaper asking for our story and allowing ten pounds sterling for a reply. This was made very brief, and made it·quite clear that we wished to avoid publicity. At Victoria can be seen the remnants of the old *Tillicum* on a grass-plot at the back of the Empress Hotel. I think it is a pity that so remarkable a vessel cannot be preserved in a better condition, for she is rapidly falling into a sad state of decay. However, for all that, she is well worth a visit. This *Tillicum* was an Indian canoe, thirty feet in length, in which Captain Voss, after many remarkable adventures, achieved an ocean passage of 40,000 miles. I believe that her owner ended his days in California, where he was a taxi-driver.

I do not think that the average Englishman knows over-much about the activities of other parts of the Empire. It is hard for him to do so, of course, when the countries which form it cover so great a portion of the earth's surface. Hence a few words about the activities of our hosts here will not be amiss. The total strength of the Royal Canadian Navy is not much over one thousand, and that is counting the east coast as well as the west. Most of their officers have been trained in various ships of the Royal Navy, to which they return at intervals, so that there are always some of them over in England, doing specialist courses or serving for a commission in one of the ships of the Fleet. The *personnel* of the lower-deck struck us as being exceptionally smart and everything was carried out with an enthusiasm which was most refreshing to witness. Their volunteer reserve seemed to have caught this same spirit, and at the time of our visit they were voluntarily attending for a fortnight's annual training, and travelling from as far afield as Winnipeg in order to do so. When I mention that this distance direct is about 1,500 miles, perhaps you will realise why their base made such a great impression on us. Their ships consisted of two destroyers, the *Vancouver* and *Skeena*, while a trawler, the *Armentières*, was also in use for training purposes.

The civilian population here were extremely friendly, and even if they do consider the Englishman a little insular, it is no very deep-rooted objection to him, as the frequent reference to his island as the " old country " will prove. Chancing to ring up on the telephone an English friend of mine at his business address in Victoria, I was answered by one of his companions, who went off to fetch him. When I next met him he seemed highly amused. I discovered that when the telephone had been answered, he had been summoned to it by being told that there was somebody " frightfully Ox-ford " who wanted to speak to him on the telephone ; and this was not the only place where different methods of intonation were to transform the English language into a veritable shibboleth of rival tongues. It is of interest to reflect that the total population of Canada is not much more than that of London at the present time.

We had carried various articles of clothing of a respect-able nature on board the vessel as far as Yokohama, where the Canadian Pacific Steamship Company took charge of them for us and kindly agreed to forward them to

Victoria to await our arrival. On the last day there,
one member of the crew had busied himself in purchasing the monkey of whose existence you have already
heard. This monkey had occasioned his owner a great
deal of concern by squatting down in the middle of one
of the busiest streets in Yokohama and declining to
move. Finally a taxi had to be procured to solve the
difficulty, and by the time the new arrival had been
signed on, his owner had omitted to place his suitcase
with the remainder. So now he found himself without
the dinner-jacket and other formal attire by which the
others were enabled to appear as quite respectable
members of society. However, the people here made
allowances, and he was able to collect the missing
articles on arrival at San Francisco.

By the time that we had arrived here we had decided
that one of the greatest improvements that could be
made would be the purchase of more reliable cooking-
stoves. The cook had found that the Chinese stoves
were impossible, and had decided that they must go.
Then it was that we heard of a Canadian product called
" Rock-Gas." Most of the yachts in those waters were
fitted with it, and had found it most satisfactory. We
needed two pretty large cylinders to contain sufficient
for our needs. We stood them up vertically and they
fitted in the spare space under the ladder leading from
the galley to the upper deck. We scrapped the old
stoves and oven, and fitted a simple gas-ring in lieu,
with double burners and a portable stove. We gym-
balled this and connected it to the gas cylinders by
copper pipes, while rubber piping formed the connec-
tion for the moving portion.

On the afternoon of Wednesday, the 27th of September, we left the Naval Barracks in tow of a Canadian naval launch. A large party of officers gathered to see us off, and we were again provided with various additions for the larder. We had a long beat out of the Juan de Fuca Straits, but, as was so often the case after a stay in harbour, we felt none too inclined for food when out in the open sea once more. We had fine, sunny weather, with northerly winds, for the first few days. The weather was so fine, in fact, that we were thoroughly enjoying it and our meals, for I quote from my diary on 5th October, the eighth day after leaving Esquimalt : " I do not know what people who imagine that one eats weevilly biscuits and salt tack would say to this actual menu of a couple of days ago : *Breakfast* : porridge, scrambled eggs and beans, coffee and unlimited fresh bread. *Lunch* : cold lobster, salad, fresh lettuce and tomatoes and German sausages. *Supper* (hot) : chicken, sausages, bacon, bread-sauce, fresh potatoes and kidney-beans. This was followed by one large and one small apple-pie with custard, and, finally coffee ! ! " We were sighting a good deal of shipping, but otherwise our daily life consisted mainly of eating and sleeping between watches. However, strange as it may seem, we managed to get along without getting bored with each other.

We had looked forward for a long time to our arrival at San Francisco and to passing through the Golden Gate. We arrived there after dark, however, on Friday, 6th October, ten days after leaving Esquimalt. We sailed up the harbour, past all the lights which showed us where work was in progress on the new bridge which is to span the harbour mouth, and of which the people of San Francisco are rightly proud. We were not very clever about our selection of an anchorage. We had intended to make for the yacht harbour, but, failing to find it, we entered another small bay which seemed to offer a good shelter for the night. Unfortunately it proved to be the berthing harbour for numerous large ferries which cross the harbour to Oakland. We were so glad to be at anchor that we finally trusted to luck and retired to bed, and the ferries must have altered course, for we were still there at daylight. We were then towed clear by the coastguard launch, which kindly came alongside for the purpose. We had rather stupidly omitted to provide ourselves with some papers at Dutch Harbour, our first American port of call, so that formalities took a longer time than usual. It also cost us a few dollars for rat harbourage inspection ; we did not have any of these vermin on board. We had accomplished a further 819 miles towards our goal, at a daily average of eighty-seven and a half miles.

One of the first people to board us was an American naval officer on the Admiral's staff, who arranged for us to be towed round to Pier 9, one of the many piers of this huge harbour. The Press representatives were soon on board and eager to have a story. We had been warned that it would be a wise plan to have a plain statement of facts already written out. We accordingly acted on this advice. The Press reporters were well satisfied with it, and the method can be recommended to others who may be contemplating a yacht visit to American ports. We were naturally very amused at one reporter who wanted to know if it was true that there were five British naval " captains " on board ! Several photographs had to be taken before these courteous but pressing individuals could be persuaded to leave us. One of the greatest delights of our arrival in harbour was the receiving of letters. A member of the Consular staff was waiting to greet us here, and brought them with him.

At that time America was still under prohibition, but it was not long before a gentleman arrived on board who had apparently managed to evade the law. He kindly took two of the crew around the town to see the sights, and they had a hectic drive in consequence. Florida, the thirty-third State to do so, had just voted against the continuance of prohibition. The hospitality was very good here, and our first afternoon we visited the University Club, the St. Francis Yacht Club, and dined at Jack's Restaurant.

Next day being Sunday, some of the crew decided to laze in bed for the morning. One of the first things that struck us was the size of the Sunday papers which, with their supplements, provided us with a good forenoon's reading. In the afternoon we received an invitation from the St. Francis Yacht Club to berth *Tai-Mo-Shan* in their magnificent yacht harbour. We gladly accepted the proffered tow and berthed close to the club late that afternoon. This club is a most luxurious place and, looking out as it does across the Golden Gate, can boast of one of the finest views of any yacht club in the world.

We had some interesting drives around this great city. We were seeing our first sky-scrapers which tower above the harbour, while large parks and fine views add to the city's grandeur. We were surprised to find that numbers of squalid buildings and small wooden bungalows were being erected on the outskirts of this impressive city. We soon learned that the inhabitants strongly object to the curtailment of the name to " 'Frisco." Numerous parties were given in our honour, and throughout our stay here the hospitality was of a very high order. Indeed, had it not been for the British Consul and his wife, who placed their house at our disposal, I think that the generosity of the people here would have seriously undermined our constitutions. We had a tremendous number of visitors to the boat, among whom was Miss Cazalet, a member of parliament.

We visited some of the many speak-easies, entrance to which seemed a comparatively easy affair. I do not think that they were really very much more exciting than the average London night club. I must own that we got quite a thrill out of being introduced to the manager of one of these many haunts. As he was advancing to shake hands with us, our friends informed us in a whisper that he was known to have had at least four people bumped off. It may not have been true, but our host's reputation certainly succeeded in giving an added interest to the interview.

An American football match was taking place, during our stay, at California University, and we were taken to see it. On the way there one of us stepped in front of a motor-car which was just coming on to the ferry. These ferries are massive affairs, with a system of parallel lanes which allows for the transport of a huge number of cars. On stepping out of your car it is advisable, as one of us learned to his cost, to step on to the dividing path and not into the next lane. However, no serious damage was done, but this member of the crew went to sea next day strapped up like an Egyptian mummy. The American football match was not one of the largest matches of that season, but at the same time immense enthusiasm was displayed by the large crowd who gathered to witness it. My impressions of the game were, very briefly, as follows, though it would be absurd to compare the merits of the game with that of Rugby football, when it would need a long and close study of the rules before they were thoroughly understood. The game is similar in many ways to Rugby football, but the play is not nearly so continuous. Eight minutes is said to be an average time during which a player is in motion during the whole game. When the players are moving, tremendous bursts of speed govern their actions. The thing that would surprise a Rugby footballer is the substitution for players of reserves, which may occur at frequent intervals throughout the game. In this game I saw eight substitutes go on the field at once, and it is not uncommon for the coach to send on the entire second team when his first team require a rest, or are having it all their own way. As you may gather, the coaches are very important people, and in leading teams can command immense salaries. Their control of the game while it is being played is enormous owing to this substitution. The ball is shaped like a Rugger ball but is sufficiently narrow to be held in the average palm ; the ground is marked off by white lines every five yards from the centre to the extremities of the field. A game lasts one hour, and, unlike Rugby football, there are only eleven players on each side. The number of serious casualties form a much higher percentage than in the English game. Apart from the field of play, the spectators play an important part. The band of each team parade before the commencement of the game, and are responsible for great enthusiasm among the organised supporters, who keep up a continuous chorus throughout the play.

Following this game we visited the California University. We were greatly impressed with the facilities for games here. There were excellent swimming-baths, gymnasiums, squash-courts and massage-rooms.

There were some amusing incidents during our stay at San Francisco. One of the larger members of the crew took some clothes to be pressed to a small shop kept by an Italian. A few days later, another member of the crew who was of smaller stature chanced to be passing that way. He called in to collect these clothes, and was surprised to be met with the remark, " Come to collect your fadder's clothes—eh ? "

Another day a pleasant old gentleman chanced on board with a youth who, he explained, was his son, who was keen on sailing. His numerous questions were answered by me, as I chanced to be on board alone. On learning that I was the cook, he was most desirous to know more particulars about the *personnel* of the vessel, and such whispered questions as " Who are they ? " " How do they treat you ? " etc. followed each other in rapid succession. He left the vessel blissfully ignorant of the true state of affairs !

We started on our way again on Sunday the 15th of October, and had a fine send-off, as, in addition to a number of the friends that we had made here, several yachts accompanied us to the harbour limits. Good weather conditions—cloudless sky, maximum visibility and slight northerly breezes—favoured us at the start. At this stage of our voyage the days' runs between Hong-Kong and San Francisco averaged only eighty-eight miles. We were not perturbed, as, though we had hoped for much higher figures, we realised that we had been following a route which was an unusual one for a sailing-boat without an engine. We felt confident that a time would come when we would have an opportunity of beating the longest day's run to date. This still stood at 196 miles, which we had done just prior to our arrival at Formosa. We had also had several individual days when we had done between 150 and 200 miles, and when the average was only lowered by the continuance of calm weather and light winds. The latter still persisted on this next leg of our voyage, which was a comparatively short one of 371 miles. That Sunday afternoon we had a fine view of the naval dirigible, *Makon*, flying low over San Francisco, as it arrived to take up its moorings there for the first time.

Pelicans were numerous now, and a fly-catcher was a passenger on board for thirty-six hours ; we calculated his consumption of moths or flies at no less than three hundred a day ! A week after leaving San Francisco we sailed into San Pedro harbour, and at an early hour passed under the bows of the United States battleship, *Florida*. Owing to these persistent light winds the passage here had seriously strained our endurance. After the usual customs formalities we were taken alongside the Wilmington Yacht Club's pontoon and were thus free to explore Hollywood, which by motor-car was but forty minutes distant.

Our daily average for this passage worked out at fifty-five miles.

CHAPTER XII

A Slow Passage Down to Mexico

Our ill-luck with the obtaining of winds favourable to swift passages from port to port cannot be said to have dogged us on arrival in harbour. Here we were again, with our boat comfortably berthed within a short distance of an excellent yacht club, of which we had the honour to be made temporary members. As had been the case a short time before at San Francisco, we made many friends during our stay here. One of the first people to greet us was the British Consul, who did such a tremendous lot to make our stay here a memorable one. We were also very keen to visit the Hollywood Film Studios, and we did not have to wait long before our wishes were fulfilled. One of the first film-companies' premises to be visited were those of the Metro-Goldwyn Mayer, or M.G.M., as they are more familiarly known. I think that it was here that one of the first things that chanced to catch the eye was a collection of technical books for reference purposes, among which *King's Regulations and Admiralty Instructions* occupied a prominent position. We were somewhat surprised to see our Naval " Bible " there, but still more so when we learned that they even have the amendments, which are published from time to time, forwarded to them. In contrast to this, an employee, who was waiting to go on the " set," and who was passing the time seated on an alligator's head, whilst reading his morning newspaper, afforded us amusement.

The following day we accompanied the others to the Fox Studios. Here we were introduced to Mr. Lasky, the eminent producer, who, though he is a very busy man, spent some time in showing us round. All these film premises cover huge areas and are self-contained, with modern buildings and restaurants. We lunched in one of these and found it most interesting. The actors and actresses came in to lunch in whatever costume their part required of them, so that one had a mixed assortment both of colour and fashion on which to feast the eye. Various celebrities of the film world were pointed out to us and added to our interest in this unique gathering. We went on to several of the " sets " and watched the films in the making. Admission to view this is harder to obtain than it was in the old days, when the talking of a visitor did not mean the spoiling of several hundred feet of film. Loud warning bells act as very efficient reminders of the necessity of keeping silence. When we stated that *Cavalcade* had not been shown in Hong-Kong before our departure, arrangements were at once made for the showing of this film. We saw it under the most comfortable conditions, in a private-demonstration theatre on the Company's premises. Outside, Trafalgar Square was still standing, and, with the other London scenery employed in this film, was so realistic that one could easily imagine oneself back in London instead of in California. We were taken in a motor-car to view the scenery used in the films. We would pass through an Irish village street, past house fronts which were perfect representations of the real thing, but behind which, if one were to look, were supports of timber and scaffolding. We would come to a large cathedral front copied in minutest detail from the original in some far-away part of the world, and then the car would take us through a squalid area, a perfect representation of a part of New York in the days gone by : and so we went on for over half-an-hour. We saw the pool in which sea-monsters can be filmed by means of cameras and lights cleverly arranged under water. We passed the park where every type of foreign tree is grown, so that it can be used when required ; and we drove back into Grosvenor Square when the sun was setting. It was just as though we were standing in that very place : the grass plot in the centre surrounded by railings, the trees, the lamp-post, the letter-box, all added to the clever delusion ; but one thing was missing—the smell of the London taxi-cabs !

There was an animal farm from which lions and other animals are hired by the film companies when required. We heard the story of an alligator and how the actor who was appearing with it was a little scared, but that when its turn came to appear, so sleepy was the animal that they had to place a block of ice on its head to awaken it.

We met a retired British naval officer one day at Hollywood. His job made him a general information bureau for the world of films. He would be rung up and asked some intricate question about the correct costume of a sailor or a soldier at some period connected with a film, or any other similar query. He had a wonderful library of reference-books and could give the correct answer in a very short time.

The film directors are very particular about details, and so it is seldom nowadays that you will notice glaring faults in any film.

We watched various scenes being shot and we were fortunate enough to meet John Barrymore, Alan Mowbray, Bette Davis, Warren William, Maureen O'Sullivan, and other famous Hollywood stars. Various cocktail parties were arranged in our honour, and throughout our stay the British Consul arranged some entertainment for us at all hours of the day. We were invited on board the warship *California* one day, and met many of their officers.

We were also fortunate enough to meet Harry Pidgeon, the veteran ocean-sailor, who was living on board his famous yawl, the *Islander*, in Los Angeles harbour. He built this boat himself and it had taken him a year and a half to complete it. She was thirty-four feet overall, ten feet nine inches beam, and had a draught of just over five feet. Sailing this small boat westward from Los Angeles, he had completed a voyage of nearly 27,000 miles. When we met him he took us down into the cabin, which was twelve feet long. It had a bunk each side and a small wood-burning stove at the aft end. He seemed to find it an ideal life, and though he was approaching seventy he told us that he shortly hoped to be setting off on his travels once more. He showed great interest in *Tai-Mo-Shan*, which, having been built under Ocean Racing Club Rules, was a very different type of boat to his own excellent little craft. Our heavy rigging necessitated by the passage through the typhoon area caused him some surprise.

It was while the boat was lying at Wilmington that we first met Larry Kent, the skipper of the *Audacious*. He showed us around a good deal and eventually proposed accompanying us in his own craft down the west coast of America. Our intentions had been to visit San Diego, which is a large naval base, and from there we had intended to do a long sea-trip direct to the Galapagos Islands, which lie some 600 miles to the westward of Panama. We had picked on them owing to the great attraction of the various strange creatures, such as giant iguanas and flightless cormorants, which make their home there. Now it was proposed that the American and the British yacht should accompany each other down the American coast. This proposal was so attractive a one that we altered our programme accordingly. In doing this, we unfortunately had to miss out our visit to San Diego. It was not until after we had made this decision that we discovered that by doing this we were missing a great reception by the American Fleet there. However, time was an important factor and, despite our regrets, we set sail from Wilmington, California, on the 1st of November. The *Audacious*, which had an engine, towed us out of San Pedro harbour and past the battleships at anchor. Referring to our departure from here, we later received the following letter, on arrival at Panama, from an American naval officer. He said :

" Gentlemen,

I have just come below after watching your little ketch slide out of port into the blue. Good luck to her !

I wish that our fleet, every ship, would have run up a signal *Bon Voyage*. We made it, but I fear you were too busy making sail to notice.

"Somehow it seems to me that you have done much for all naval officers, and those of us who cannot share your adventure look on with admiration and regret. In our 'Naval Institute' a yachtsman friend wrote a paper entitled 'Are there any Sailors in the Navy?' You have answered better than a bottle of ink or a whole battery of typewriters.

"For myself and for every man who loves ships and the sea, and knows what adventure and satisfaction your voyage means, let me say again, Good Luck.

Sincerely,
Etc."

When we received this letter we felt gratified that, in these days when the sailor has to be an adept at working intricate machinery and instruments, the fact that seamanship must still play an important part had not been overlooked.

As soon as we were clear of the harbour we hoisted our sails, and both vessels set their course for Acapulco, which was to be our next stop. A third yacht followed astern, as she was *en route* to San Diego. A good wind at the start gave us the lead, and we left both the other yachts well astern. In the evening our friend in the *Audacious* started up his engine and came up with us. The wind falling light, we accepted his offer of a tow, and we continued thus throughout the night. This was not the only time that we availed ourselves of his engine, but it was a practice which was not to prove altogether practicable. Our change of route necessitated a great deal of sailing through areas noted for their calms. However, we soon found that any swell caused a heavy strain on the engine, due to the suddenness of the load imposed on it. We therefore arranged a rendezvous some two hundred miles ahead, and when the wind allowed of it we proceeded under sail. This cruising together over such long distances was a most interesting experience. As we passed San Diego we much regretted our inability to call in there, but luckily we sighted some destroyers who were out exercising. By means of our Aldis lamp, which is a signalling device used aboard warships, we were soon in communication with them and were thus able to express our regret at being unable to enjoy a visit to San Diego.

Cruising in company was not as easy of achievement as we had previously anticipated. The *Audacious* was cutter-rigged and had heavier proportions than our own boat.

To allow for our varying speeds under the changing weather conditions which we were experiencing, and also for the fact that one had an engine while the other was entirely dependent on sail, we had arranged the rendezvous. This was at the northern end of Cerros Island in Sebastian Viscaino Bay, off Lower California. We were here on Monday, 6th November, our sixth day at sea. *Audacious* had slipped the tow three days previously and, while we were hoisting our sails, had forged ahead. A fog sprang up a short time after this, and in consequence we had parted company and had not seen each other since then. Our search for our friends had its amusing side. We arrived off the northern end of the island in the early morning. We saw no sign of the *Audacious*. We thought that it was unlikely that they could be astern of us, as she had taken the lead at the beginning, and that they would in all probability have made use of their engine during the fog. We had just decided to sail to the other end of the island when the wind dropped completely. We were unable to use our wireless, as they had no operator on board their vessel. Somebody with a working knowledge of wireless, semaphore and flashing on board each vessel would be a great asset to two or more yachts wishing to do an ocean cruise together. Great enjoyment could be had in this way, and, from experience gained on this cruise, I can confidently state that a few months of concentration before starting will ensure complete proficiency. In our case the generosity of both the local Hong-Kong amateur wireless experts and Marconi's saved us the expense of installing the sets. However, owing to the great use to which wireless is now put, the consequent reduction in the price of the necessary equipment should mean but a moderate outlay to ensure a great amount of added pleasure.

All the next night we remained becalmed off the northern end. We drifted close to the island under a starry sky ; the moonlight scintillated on the ripples, which now and again were rudely disturbed by the enthusiastic leaping of some seals. Meanwhile their comrades ashore kept up the incessant roar from the rocks which had ceased as abruptly at daylight as it had started at sundown on the previous evening.

On Tuesday, 7th November, a favourable breeze allowed us to search the bays of this island for any signs of the *Audacious*. Presently we noticed some small huts ashore, and decided to find out whether they were inhabited, and, if so, whether our friend had passed by. The difficulty of discovering this would have been increased, of course, had he chanced to have passed their settlement during the night. We got busy assembling our little canvas boat. The hull was lashed just abaft the breakwater, while the two wooden ribs which kept the canvas taut when in the shape of a boat, rather on the principle of a camp-bed, were kept overhead in the saloon. The floor-boards were also stowed with them and were made so that they just passed through the hatch when the sliding roof was fully open. It was not long before we had the boat floating in the water. This boat was most satisfactory and kept remarkably dry, though it is not certain whether it would have proved suitable for landing among reefs. When all was ready, two of the crew pulled in to the beach. Here they were met by some Japanese fishermen. Though conversation had mainly to be carried on by signs, it was established that a yacht had passed by, two days previously. We got under way once more and made for the southern end of the island. Not finding her here, we finally set our course for Acapulco. A stiff breeze at the start filled us with renewed confidence, but, as was to be the rule rather than the exception, it had dropped to a flat calm by nightfall.

By noon on Wednesday, 8th November, we had travelled 323 miles since leaving Wilmington, which left us with about 1,200 miles still to do before reaching Acapulco. We were six days out, so that at this period we were averaging about fifty miles a day. On our first night after leaving this island we met a steamer, to whom we signalled. As she was coming up from the southward, we were able to establish the fact that the *Audacious* was ahead of us and probably about 100 miles away. We knew that each vessel must have thought that the other had gone on. We were all rather worried that, with persistent light winds in which he would be using his engine, he would gain such a lead on us as to make his waiting for us at Acapulco too long a business to be practicable.

A series of days of hot sun, light winds, rippling, calm seas, ending with starry, moonlit nights, followed each other with monotonous regularity. We were getting great amusement from the wireless broadcasting programmes, which helped to relieve the irritation which we felt at the continuance of light winds. One evening the helmsman was sitting with some headphones in position which were joined to the set through a round hole cut in the for'd end of the cockpit. It was one of the calm, still nights of which I have already spoken. The sails flapped idly in the light airs and added to the drowsiness which even the broadcast tunes were failing to dispel. Suddenly all was changed. The name *Tai-Mo-Shan* awakened him with a start, and his wild yell made the other four rush to the loud-speaker in the saloon. It was coming from the " Paris Inn Café " at Hollywood. They referred to our recent patronage, and after wishing both the American and British yachts a great *entente*, they announced that their next tune was to be dedicated to us. We listened to the soft, dreamy music on this perfect evening. Is it any wonder that our thoughts turned to the marvels of modern progress ? Here we were, in a small boat four hundred miles from the gaiety in which we had joined a short time previously, but listening to it under most comfortable conditions as we lay in our bunks. Unless it shall be purposely sought after, that solitude which must have proved one of the most trying character-istics of expeditions of old has been eradicated, never to return. Only quite recently this was brought home to me in a rather striking fashion. We were pursuing our way across the Atlantic at the time. One morning, I was lying on my bunk and reading at random from a book about the early explorers in Arctic waters, and chanced to read of the privations and hardships of a party who were forced to winter on Wrangel Island, which lies north of the Lena River, in Siberia. Later, on the same day, I picked up an English newspaper which we had obtained at Bermuda. As coincidence would have it, my eye chanced on the words " Wrangel Island." I read on. Again a party were suffering from the hardships of the weather conditions and a shortage of food. In contrast to those pioneers who had pre-ceded them, they were able to send out wireless distress signals. The paper account went on to describe how an aeroplane had flown to them with provisions and had taken off a large proportion of them and a quantity of furs. The remainder, doubtless, were to be picked up at a later date in similar fashion.

It would take a braver hand than mine to comment further, but there is one comforting thought to those who like to escape from the hustle and bustle of this modern witchcraft. That the wide places of the ocean can never be crowded by jostling humanity fills one with unspeakable gratitude.

During these calm days life was most peaceful, and the interior of *Tai-Mo-Shan* improved enormously. We lay in our bunks, reading, or basked in the sun. It got rather too hot for enjoyment in the middle of the day. As a general rule we were not moving during the day, but made our progress by taking advantage of the land and sea breezes. These gave us headway in the evening from about sunset until midnight, and after a calm middle watch we would again get the wind until about half-past eight. For the remainder of the day we usually got scarcely any at all.

Here is what my own diary records at this period. For Saturday, 11th November (we had left our last port on 1st November), it says : " We are stealing slowly past Magdalena Bay, close to which we had fixed our second rendezvous with *Audacious*. I *was* still optimistic, but I fear that by now he must have gone on, though I cannot believe that he still thinks that we are ahead of him, with these light winds. We saw our first Frigate Bird to-day, and, in addition to seeing two sharks, we were followed for a long time by a seal, whose curiosity was aroused by our log, which was trailing astern.

" To-day was another glorious day, which we spent basking in the sun, and by sunset we were sliding slowly past San Lazaro lighthouse. Through my glasses I could see the lighthouse-keeper, his wife, two children, two goats and some chickens. From the lighthouse they did not have a very good view inshore, as behind them was a great wall of volcanic rock. Several ' flights ' (I am not sure whether this is the correct term) of pelicans flew past, and one large line of about twenty wheeled over our heads in line abreast formation. Unwittingly they were the cause of much merriment aboard our vessel, for their expressions as they literally looked down their noses at us from above gave to them a most ludicrous appearance.

"We have just had supper of Clam Chowder and cherry-tart. The cook is getting fat, through taking an extra share of the victuals, presumably. There is no room to run round this deck, so he will have to let his figure pursue its natural course !

"*Sunday,* 12th *November.*

"Another peaceful day, with a little more wind. We now hope to catch *Audacious* at Acapulco, as she must have gone on, and should be there by now.

To Noon			Day's Run	Noon Position	
Friday, Nov.		3rd	75'.0	30° 51' N.	116° 50' W.
Sat.	,,	4th	83'.0	29° 35' N.	116° 13' W.
Sun.	,,	5th	62'.0	28° 45' N.	115° 30' W.
Mon.	,,	6th	27'.0	28° 24' N.	115° 12' W.
Tues.	,,	7th	26'.0	28° 00' N.	115° 12' W.
Wed.	,,	8th	50'.0	27° 12' N.	115° 01' W.
Thurs.	,,	9th	53'.0	26° 32' N.	114° 22' W.
Friday	,,	10th	71'.0	25° 33' N.	113° 39' W.
Sat.	,,	11th	73'.0	24° 54' N.	112° 30' W.
Sun.	,,	12th	52'.0	24° 08' N.	112° 02' W.

"Everybody has got spring-cleaning mania, owing to this calm weather, except myself.

"9 p.m., *Monday,* 13th *November.*

"Uneventful day. This is a marvellously peaceful existence ; weather conditions the same again, with less wind. Saw our first turtle.

" *Saturday, 18th November.*

" We have been making successful days' runs up to now, when wind really seems to be holding better. Up to noon to-day we have done 117 miles for our day's run. We had some excitement yesterday afternoon, when we sighted a large fin on the port side. Its owner must apparently have been dozing, as, despite our proximity, he remained there ; it was probably the dorsal fin of a Sail fish. When they are under way this fin is folded into a groove provided for the purpose. Shortly after this we fired at some porpoises with the .303 rifle. We evidently scored a bull's-eye, for one of them leaped out of the water, returning to his element again with a mighty thud. We had an argument as to whether they were large porpoises or small whales. In any case we had lost the animal, so I doubt whether we will try this means any more, as it only wounds them and they ' sound ' before anything can be done about it.

" Not long after this I saw some large fish rising fairly close to our tracks, and no sooner had I manned the line, trolling astern, than I felt a nice healthy heave. Unfortunately I had the line caught in between my toes, which hampered my movements, and finally resulted in finding me with a mere line and swivel but no wire trace or hooks.

" A little later, we noticed a shark swimming close under our stern, with three pilot fish leading the way. They swam a zig-zag course which the shark followed exactly. They had stationed themselves just under the tip of his nose. They are a fine bluey-green colour and have three dark bands across their backs. We tempted

him with some Bologna sausage, but he was too wise
to risk a naval shark-hook.

"For several days we have had a fly-catcher on
board. I have never seen a bird so tame, probably due
to hunger. He has been very fond of the coconut-oil
which is kept in a petrol-tin in the cockpit. It has a
slight leak and he has been constantly imbibing it. A
swallow joined him yesterday, but was very exhausted
to start with, and eventually pegged out, perched on
the tin, while the fly-catcher took his fill quite un-
perturbed. However, a short while ago the latter,
much to our sorrow, also went the way of all flesh by
getting strangled in the traveller on the port spinnaker
boom !

"We are well past Cape Corrientes and now the
smoke from the volcano de Safa is in sight on the port
beam.

To Noon			Noon Position	
Mon. 13th Nov.	43 miles		23° 40′ N.	111° 27′ W.
Tues. 14th ,,	53 ,,		23° 02′ N.	110° 46′ W.
Wed. 15th ,,	31 ,,		22° 11′ N.	109° 40′ W.
Thurs. 16th ,,	61 ,,		21° 37′ N.	108° 46′ W.
Fri. 17th ,,	74 ,,		21° 09′ N.	107° 34′ W.
Sat. 18th ,,	117 ,,		19° 44′ N.	106° 09′ W.

"It is warming up—to-day's noon temperatures
were :

Air	-	-	-	-	83° Fahrenheit
Wet Bulb	-	-	-	79°	,,
Sea	-	-	-	-	78° ,, ,,

This diary was kept at sea, whatever the weather,
which at times occasioned me a good deal of worry.
However, by wedging myself into a corner, I found

that it was quite possible to keep it going throughout the trip. Before setting out on this expedition, efforts to record the daily doings in diary form had started off well, but after getting shorter and shorter, the entries had always ceased abruptly by the end of February. On this trip, however, we had all found that we were already reminded of incidents which had occurred at an earlier stage in the voyage, and we were quite pleased that we had kept it going. In fact, two large volumes were filled before we lowered the sails for the last time.

In addition to our own journals we kept a ship's log, which is now a relic of our trip of a rather more formal nature. We recorded in that the direction and force of the wind, the barometer, and information of a similar character. We also noted the shifting of sail, which in these variable wind areas necessitated numerous entries which form rather solemn reading. Reproduced below is an actual page from the ship's log at this stage of our passage between San Pedro and Acapulco.

We were also keeping a Meteorological Log in which we entered up the wind, the weather, the cloud formations, the sea and swell, and, in fact, we registered all details of this nature. We did this every four hours throughout the twenty-four, and so it formed a very complete weather record. In addition to its use to meteorological experts it served to keep us busy. We were frequently asked such questions as, " Whatever do you do all the time ? " As I have explained already, we were in watch-and-watch—that is, two of us kept turn about with the two others, while Ryder was kept fully occupied taking and working out his navigational predictions. We were not finished when our watches

COPY OF PAGE OF LOG

Tuesday, Nov. 14th, 1933.

Log of the ss. *Tai-Mo-Shan* from San Pedro to Acapulco.

Hour A.M.	Speed Kts.		Course	Compass Error	Wind	Bar. and Ther.	Patent Log	Remarks
1	1	2	E. × S.½S.				712.5	
2	1	8	,,				714.3	0130 Gybed to Port Tack. 0200 Set Mizzen Staysail.
3	3	0	,,				717.3	
4	3	8	,,		N.N.E. 1	30.08°, 70°	721.1	
5	4	2	E.S.E.				725.3	0430 Handed Spinnaker. Set Jib and Forestay Sail.
6	5	6	,,				730.9	
7	6	3	,,				737.2	0630 Handed Mizzen Staysail. 0700 Set Mizzen Staysail.
8	4	1	,,		E. 1	30.10°, 74°	741.3	
9	2	2	,,				743.5	
10	0	5	,,				744.0	0915 Handed Mizzen Staysail.
11	0	5	,,				744.5	
12	0	5	E. × S.		S.E. × S. 1	30.12°, 80°	745.0	1140 Handed Spinnaker. Set headsails. FullandBye Starboard Tack Co. E.

COPY OF PAGE OF LOG—*contd.*

Position at Noon	{ By Account „ Obsn. or Bearings	23° 02′ N. 110° 46′ W.	Course and distance run 136° 53′	Bearing of Headland or Port West of C. San Lucas

Hour P.M.	Speed Kts.		Course	Compass Error	Wind	Bar and Ther.	Patent Log	Remarks
1	1	0	E.×S.				746.0	
2	2	4	E.				748.4	
3	1	4	N.E.×E.½E.				749.8	
4	4	4	N.E.×E.		S.E.×E. 3	30.06°, 82°	754.2	1600 Tacked FullandBye Co. S.½E.
5	4	8	S.×E.				759.0	1610 Handed Jib Topsail.
6	4	0	S.×E.½E.				763.0	
7	5	5	S.E.×S.				768.5	
8	3	5	S.E.×E.½E.		N.E. 1-2	30.11°, 79°	772.0	1930 Set Jib Topsail.
9	4	8	E.×S.½S.				776.8	2030 Set Mizzen Staysail.
10	7	0	,,				783.8	
11	4	2	,,				788.0	
12	3	0	,,		N.W. 1	30.14°, 77°	791.0	2400 Cape San Lucas bearing 014°.

came to an end, for we also had the meals to prepare, the weather reports to be received on the wireless, and constant repairs to ropes, wires and sails to be attended to. Indeed, one was very glad to climb into one's bunk and not at all pleased should one be disturbed by the cry, " All hands on deck ! " As a further precaution in case of emergency a loud electric horn could be operated by the helmsman, which awakened one in no uncertain manner, and by its raucous note made pretence of not having heard it quite an impossibility.

During the last week of this passage it began to get very hot by day, but the nights were cool, which allowed for a good sleep. We had great fun among the turtles, which were becoming a common sight. We had no difficulty in manœuvring our vessel within range of those who were idly drifting in company. We shot one which we later recovered, and hoisted aboard by means of tackles which we hastily rigged up for the purpose. I got busy with my knives, while the doctor was examining the internal arrangements of the animal. The nerve reactions of turtles are extraordinary, and though this one was undoubtedly stone-dead when we got him on board, his mouth and flippers continued to be a source of danger for some time. The subsequent soup and stew were a great success, the meat being tender and the juice excellent. The best way of making the soup is by cutting up the shell which covers the under-side of the animal. This part is soft and melts easily. The steaks, which should be cut off the shoulders, have to be thoroughly well pounded to obtain the best results. There are three kinds of turtle : the " loggerhead," the " hawksbill " and the well-known green turtle which supplies the soup for famous banquets. The latter has green-coloured fat and is larger than the hawksbill. The loggerhead can be distinguished from the latter by the five or more paired plates on the back compared to the hawksbill's four. Ours was a loggerhead, a variety which is not usually supposed to be of great commercial value, though we greatly appreciated this change in our diet. When we had had the remnants of turtle-steak minced up, we caught an eight-pound bonito, a fish which belongs to the same family as the mackerel. We caught this fish on the troll-line, which we always had over the stern in these waters. In the gullet of this fish were two complete John Dories, two-and-a-half inches in length. These bonitos, like the tunnies and albacores, which belong to the same family, are most remarkably built. They have streamlined bodies and pointed heads with close-fitting jaws, while inside we found that their heart, lungs, etc. are all placed in the head. This arrangement allows plenty of space for muscles, which is, I suppose, why they are the fastest fish known.

The heat began to get very trying as we neared Acapulco, and it was so hot during the day that we were compelled to spend our off-watch periods below deck. At night we slept on the upper deck. We had seen no ships close at hand for some time.

Here is a diary extract for Wednesday, 22nd November :

" A very sultry day, as a storm threatened us for some time and there was an excellent display of lightning this evening. The hurried removal of bedding from the upper deck proved unnecessary, as it has left us alone. The petrol-generator had to be taken to pieces to-day, owing to worn bearings, so B— and P— had a rather tiring day of it. We hope to clear up this last 200 miles by Saturday. Dolphins and swordfish are numerous now. Very sticky as soon as wind drops. All our Christmas cards are ready at last for despatch at Acapulco ; I think our friends will be surprised to be getting them this year. The bonito that we caught yesterday tasted good, but, like most of these tropical fish, does not taste nearly so good as the more humble

E

herring or mackerel, in my opinion. Am removing all bones before dishing them up, but do not want this to serve as a precedent ! It is bound to become pretty uncomfortable when we are beating against the head winds in the Caribbean, and I shall not feel quite so willing then, I'm thinking ! "

On Sunday morning, 26th November, after twenty-six days at sea, we reached Acapulco on the western coast of Mexico. We had covered 1,531 miles, at a daily average of fifty-eight miles.

CHAPTER XIII

Adventures in Mexico

Acapulco is a small Mexican town with white-walled houses surrounding a pretty little bay with numerous bathing-beaches. Since we left there an earthquake has visited the place and done serious damage. As we rounded the last headland on that Sunday morning, we were delighted to sight the *Audacious* anchored close inshore. We anchored near them, and had a big reunion-party with our friends. It was baking-hot, once we had anchored, and we spent a great deal of the day on board the other yacht, where we had the advantage of awnings. Ashore, the small hotels surrounded the public square, in which most of the population seemed to have gathered to laze away the day. In fact, so great was the heat that we felt perfectly satisfied to sit outside the café and sip iced drinks, while we watched the inhabitants, who strolled or lounged about, in wide-brimmed hats and with pistols on their hips. It being a Sunday, the formalities connected with our arrival were deferred until the following morning. It is not wise to clear from or arrive at a Mexican port on a Sunday, as it may entail double the usual charges to allow for the disturbance which one is causing to the officials, and Mexicans are particularly fond of their Sunday sleep.

The following morning we visited the " Aduana,"

or Customs House, armed with a pile of documents. It was a most tiring morning, as the speed at which Spanish was spoken added to the complications of some very lengthy explanations about the purposes of our visit. When we had hoped that all was satisfactorily completed, a new difficulty seemed to have arisen and resulted in the production of a large, official-looking tome. These were the Customs Regulations and quite defeated the restricted knowledge of the language which we possessed. The services of an interpreter were finally procured.

It then was explained to us that on the arrival of a merchant-ship an official had to be placed on board. The large tome was pointed to as evidence of the fact, though we were willing to accept it without further query. The official had been on board our vessel since our arrival, and so we were surprised when the matter still seemed to be unsolved. After a long and excited conversation between the harassed officials and the man who had been procured to act as interpreter, it was explained to us what the trouble was about. It appeared that the guard placed on board *Tai-Mo-Shan* had complained that he was not provided with meals. As cook of *Tai-Mo-Shan*, I grew as excited as my meagre command of his language would allow, and asserted my willingness to provide a suitable sum of money in lieu of food, owing to my keen desire to rest from my labours while in harbour. This resulted in further regulations, and in vain did we explain that we were not a merchant-ship but a yacht on pleasure bound. The forenoon was well advanced before a sum suitable for placating the hungry official had been agreed upon. It is strongly advisable for a yachting enthusiast who may be wishing to visit this exciting country to provide himself with a document clearly stating that his vessel is a yacht and that he is visiting the country for pleasure. This statement, if signed by some good authority such as his yacht club, should save him endless trouble.

That afternoon we refreshed ourselves by motoring out to Pié de la Cuesta, where on one side the road is bounded by a large lagoon, while on the seaward side a sandy beach stretches for over one hundred miles. This trip was only a few miles, but we began to realise what an interesting country we were visiting. We saw blue herons, wild parrots, and flocks of revolting buzzards called zopilotes. These great birds have black bodies, against which their blood-red faces stand out in striking contrast. When they are on their scavenging expeditions they cover the ground in great leaps, which add to the weirdness of their appearance. A young child stopped us to show us her plaything. It was a young crocodile, and we were glad to see that its business end was secured with string !

We made preparations for a flight to Mexico City the following day. Next morning our two friends from the *Audacious* joined the five of us, and we boarded the 'plane, which was an old Fokker. Mexico City was some 250 miles away, and we flew over a continuous series of mountain ranges. The twin mountains of Popacatapetl and Ixtaccihuatl, which means "A Sleeping Woman," to which this mountain bears a striking resemblance, were a magnificent sight. The first-named, whose summit was covered with snow, is some

18,000 feet in height. Mexico City itself is 7,500 feet above sea-level, and when we reached there about 1.30 p.m. our landing speed was between eighty and 100 miles per hour. We were somewhat relieved when we finally got there, as the party and baggage had caused the machine to be somewhat overloaded. The nature of the country over which these pilots have to fly their machines must call for exceptional skill should an emergency landing ever prove necessary. Two young Mexican aviators had been killed in collision between their 'planes that morning.

We all put up at the Plaza Hotel in Mexico City in close proximity to some fine public gardens which are very similar to those in London. While in Mexico City we were to meet many of the upper classes who had received their education in England or America. As foreign medical and other degrees are no longer recognised, the numbers of those who receive their education abroad will be considerably less in the future than in the past. There are a multitude of things to be seen in this interesting city with a population of over a million souls. There are scores of churches and museums, but perhaps outstanding in interest, owing to its unusual nature, is the National Pawn-Shop. This was founded in 1775 by the owner of some fabulously rich mines, for the purpose of loaning money at a low rate of interest to less fortunate people upon their personal property, and thus save them from the high rate of interest charged by the pawnbrokers.

We drove out to Teotihuacan, which means " Place where deities are worshipped," and saw the Pyramids to the Sun and the Moon, the Temple of Quetzalcoatl and the Stadium. These buildings are several thousand years old and their origin is as yet unknown. The Pyramid of the Sun measures 761 feet across the base, which is larger than the better-known Egyptian pyramids. The structures have been built at several times, the older ones having been covered by newer ones, while the latest ones were abandoned for unknown reasons. I was most impressed with the wonderful state of preservation of some of these dwelling-houses where, despite their immense age, the original blue and pink paint is still as good as ever in places. There was even a recess in one of the walls where the primitive man had stood for a shower-bath while the water was drawn from a well close by and then poured through a hole at the top of this recess. Further excavations are proceeding now, with interesting results.

It was a hot afternoon and our sight-seeing had made us thirsty. We stopped at a small village inn. We sampled tequila, mezcal and pulque, drinks made from various portions of the cactus plant. Even the fact that one of them is the juice of the root which is sucked up out of the latter and then ejected into a pig's bladder for storing did not lessen our enjoyment at sampling them that afternoon. The custom of sucking a lime or some salt after swallowing the drink has a pleasant effect.

We visited Guadalupe on the way home, which possesses the most sacred shrine in Mexico. Legend has it that on this spot the Virgin converted an Indian's rough cloth into a beautiful cloth bearing her image. This church was built in 1695, and the cloth is enclosed in a frame of gold and surrounded by a solid silver railing weighing fourteen tons. We saw the worshippers advancing on their knees up the aisle. Up till recently a pilgrimage was carried out annually in this manner from Mexico City three miles away, but the practice has now been stopped by the Government.

We also included the remarkable " floating gardens " of Xochimilco in our sight-seeing expeditions on another day. These gardens, at the time that Cortes sacked the city of Xochimilco (" place of flowers "), floated about on twigs and were moved around as desired by the Indian gardeners. In the course of time they became attached to the bottom of the lake and are now intersected by miles of waterway. Modern invention has of course intervened here and, owing to the limited time at our disposal, we had to avail ourselves of it. I refer to the motor-boats which can now be hired to traverse these waterways, though the more romantic-minded can still hire a gondola, in which meals and wine can be accompanied by the sweet strains of a guitar.

In the evening there was as much amusement to be had as in any other large city. Some of it was out of the ordinary. There was the game of " Jai Lai," or " Pelota " as it is known in Spanish countries. This game is played in a large court and is slightly similar to rackets on a grander scale. The players have to be trained from their youth, as the speed of the game is terrific. Then there was the Gran Plaza de Gallos—or cockfights—to be visited. These were accompanied by much betting, and attracted a pretty rough crowd. On Sunday afternoon we accompanied the rest of the inhabitants of Mexico City, or so it seemed, to the bull-fights.

Did you enjoy it ? Is it cruel ? Aren't the horses a

pathetic sight ? etc.—is what one is usually asked by those of one's own countrymen who have not had the opportunity of visiting a bull-fight themselves. This was not the first occasion on which I had witnessed this form of sport. Frequent opportunities of doing so occur in Spanish cities, where the procedure is the same. I shall set down my impressions of the scene, though everybody requiring more detailed information on this controversial subject should read *Death in the Afternoon*, by Ernest Hemingway.

I enjoyed both this series of fights and those that I had witnessed previously, for one is bound to get a thrill out of being among a crowd of some sixty or seventy thousand of the people whose country one is visiting. They got worked up to a fever pitch of enthusiasm and their songs and shouting added to the general excitement. A hat seized from its unfortunate owner's head would be slung around the packed auditorium and would be joined by a score or more. Yes, I own to having been thrilled even before the first bull came rushing into the ring. It was then full of life and strength—strength which it proceeded to spend in chasing its human opponents into their funk-holes, formed by small wooden partitions behind which the matadors are safe. Next, the matador made the animal spend his strength still more by passing him with his cape, to and fro, while he himself executed most graceful turns.

The next stage is perhaps the one with which I find it hard to be in sympathy. By this time the bull's strength is, or should be, a little spent, but not sufficiently for the matador to complete his task. The bull must be weakened still more. We watched him standing in the arena, his frothy muzzle and heaving flanks bearing testimony to the rage which was consuming him. Then a horse was led in close to the boards which separated him from the front row of spectators. The bull did not seem to notice the new arrival. The horse was mercifully blindfolded and its body was well padded. Any gruesome spectacle is therefore avoided to-day, except in the mind of the imaginative spectator.

The horse was led to a point close to the bull. They turned him towards the beast. The bull seemed to come to a quick decision. He lowered his head and with a rush he placed his horns under the belly of the horse. The picador chose this moment to thrust the point of his short spear-like weapon into the bull's shoulders. Three times he was allowed to do this, but by the laws of bull-fighting, should he fail to strike home, it counted as one of his three attempts. We saw the bull lift horse and rider bodily. The rider was often unseated, and an interesting, though pathetic, fact is that the horse invariably does his best to protect the rider from the bull. The reward of these faithful animals is usually death outside, if not inside, the ring. Their owner gets the proud sum of fifteen pesos, approximately fifteen shillings.

When the rider was on the ground the matador's assistants, the banderilleros, hurried to the scene and waved their caps frantically, to distract the attention of the animal and so avert disaster. After the third " pic," each of the six bulls that we saw that afternoon was a changed animal from the one that had entered the ring a short time previously. He stood snorting in the centre of the arena, a large patch of blood staining his black shoulders.

The banderilleros were the next to deal with the infuriated animal. Each matador has two of these assistants. They approached the bull cautiously, poising aloft two gaily-decorated yard-length sticks. These are known as " banderilleras." When they had judged that the moment was the correct one, they darted in at lightning speed and thrust the points into the shoulders of the bull. Often they failed in their attempts, and then we saw perhaps one, or even both of these banderilleras fall to the ground. When both were correctly placed, we watched the bull shaking and writhing in a mad attempt to rid himself of them, while his tail lashed from side to side with fury. The banderilleros next performed a certain amount of cape-work which enabled the matador to gauge the habits of the animal that he was about to fight.

Then came the final stage. The matador, with concentrated coolness and courage, faced the bull and flaunted a muleta in front of it. His balance and poise were remarkable, as the horn of the beast passed within an inch of his body. His suit weighed eighteen pounds, thus steadying him in his movements where a slip would have meant a severe wounding, or even death. As he performed a pass of exceptional daring the spectators bellowed their admiration, and, to still further mark their appreciation of his skill, hats were flung into the arena. He turned his back in the face of the bull and bowed his gratitude.

The rushes of the animal seemed to be getting shorter and more feeble. Twice the matador shook the bull by the horns, twice he kicked him, and often he turned his back on the animal while he bowed to his frantically-excited admirers. The bull, as if answering this challenge, charged again, but its effort ended in its sinking on its knees. It was a relief when the Volapié, that is a safe and easy kill, was administered by the idol of the crowd.

The band blared forth, but was almost drowned by the enthusiasm of the huge crowd. The doors by which the animal had entered the arena swung open, and in came two very gaily-decorated mules. The chains that they dragged behind them were hitched to the body of the animal. As it rolled and bumped over the surface of the very ground on which it had but a few moments before been displaying its immense strength, I felt that it was a pity that its appearance in the ring had to end in death.

As the gates closed on the sixth and last bull to meet its fate that Sunday afternoon, we rose from our seats with mixed feelings. As we did so, we noticed the matador walking round the edge of the arena, returning the hats to his admirers.

That evening we decided to return by easy stages to Acapulco and the sea once more. We motored from Mexico City down to Cuernavaca, which lies some 4,500 feet above sea-level. Next morning the view that greeted us was a wonderful one. The town of Cuernavaca is made most attractive by the masses of red and purple bougainvillea which grow there. Other many-coloured flowers and birds of brilliant plumage add to its charm, but crowning all this beauty are the twin snow-capped peaks of Popacatapetl and Ixtaccihuatl.

From Mexico City to Acapulco, the Mexican port on the Pacific coast, is 280 miles, and as Cuernavaca is only forty-five miles from the capital we still had over 200 miles to do. We spent the night at Cuernavaca, and set off next morning by car for Acapulco. We stopped for lunch at Taxco, which has a church with a striking tile dome, the whole being a gift of a Frenchman named Joseph de la Borda, who made millions in the mining industry here.

Our impressions of this motor-drive were of continuous mountain ranges, ranches, giant cactuses, twisty, dusty dirt roads and numerous haciendas or large farms, each with their own church, but most of them had been in a dilapidated condition since the revolution. At Taxco I counted ten churches in addition to the cathedral, and its population was only just over 4,000 inhabitants. At 7 p.m., after a few stops, we had reached Chilpancingo, some 4,700 feet above sea-level, leaving us with about ninety miles to complete our journey. By this time the clothes which had been suitable at 7,500 feet caused us to feel extremely hot ; in addition to this we were very dusty and tired, so we called a halt here.

As some of the party were keen to get back to the vessels, an additional car was procured, and two members remained behind. This arrangement resulted in a terrible night. Earlier in the afternoon we had given a lift to a man who had stopped us on the road. Apparently he was not altogether unknown at Taxco, for when we stopped there we were warned by a silversmith to look after any valuables that we might have on our persons. Meanwhile the American whose company I was sharing was not keen to journey to Acapulco unless a policeman accompanied us. As my one ambition was to get back to *Tai-Mo-Shan*, I readily agreed to his proposals, more especially after noting the hungry look on the face of our travelling companion when he saw the twenty-dollar bills which my friend carried with him. We finally set off at 10 p.m., and while the policeman sat with the driver in front, we shared the stranger's company in the back. We had gone about a mile downhill in much less than the proverbial minute, when we ran over an unfortunate dog. Instead of decreasing the speed, we seemed to have become possessed of the same devil that had caused the dog to meet its fate at our hands. By this time my companion was asleep, but noticing the stranger who was with us, sleep did not come so readily to me. I smoked innumerable cigarettes while we executed the most amazing manœuvres in escaping cows, goats, donkeys and pot-holes.

At the small village of Papagayo I agreed with the policeman's suggestion that we should have some coffee and scrambled eggs. It was then well past midnight, but even at that hour a group of Mexican Indians sat drinking sequila. It was here that I confided to my American friend the mistrust in which I held the " man in the corner." As I was the less sleepy of the two, it was agreed that I should take charge of the dollar bills, which amounted to a handsome sum. I slipped round to the back of the car and proceeded to check the amount. I noticed our friend of the corner eyeing me round the hood. This finally put me on my guard. We had a further stop of over an hour while we waited for oil, in search of which the policeman disappeared from view. It was 3 a.m. before we finally reached Acapulco, where our friend of the corner disappeared into the darkness, and we paid off the car, which returned with the policeman from whence it had come. In fact it had vanished from sight, and I was congratulating myself on having kept our funds safe, when my American friend said, " Say, that damned guy has pinched my watch ! "

The next day was spent in making the necessary preparations for putting to sea once more, and on Wednesday, 6th December, after nine days in harbour, the two yachts weighed their anchors.

CHAPTER XIV

By Way of Salvador to Panama

A couple more hands were signed on in *Audacious*. Up to this time there had been the skipper, his cousin, and three paid hands, but now an American man and his wife joined them. They were seeking work and were glad of this trip down the coast. For the first two days it was very hot and the sea was so calm that we were glad of the tow which took us well clear of the land. After this a " Norther " sprang up and both boats sailed out across the bay instead of following the coast, as we had been doing. We soon drew ahead of *Audacious* at a speed of six and a half knots across the Gulf of Tehuantapec. Calm periods alternated with moderate breezes, and though we were in tow when the wind failed, we soon found that the engine was beginning to feel the strain. We had a load of petrol on board as a reserve for the *Audacious* engine, but on the sixth day we decided to transfer it to his vessel, as we had decided to give up attempts at towing and join up together at La Libertad. We were getting anxious again about the calms here, which are famous on this portion of the west coast. Our last mail had been received two months earlier and we were not expecting our next batch of letters until our arrival at Panama. This trip was but a short one, so on Monday, 11th December, when the wind dropped but left a confused sea, the American yacht bade us farewell and "mo-tored" off in the direction of La Libertad. We made a good fight with a fish here. The middle-watchman felt the troll line at about 2 a.m. and found that there was something pretty lively on the end of it. He hauled it up to the stern, and had just dropped it into the cock-pit, when, despite the darkness, he realised by its struggles that it was clear of the hooks. He seized one of the heavy reefing-spanners and aimed his blows as best he could. Next morning some heavy dents in the wooden deck bore witness to the struggle. It proved to be a five-foot barracuda. These fish can attain a length of eight feet and are most ferocious : they have the most vicious jaws armed with long, sharp teeth. Certain species are poisonous, but as others are excellent eating we wanted to try this one I settled the matter by boiling a small piece of silver with a portion of the fish, and as the silver did not tarnish, I assured the others that it would be non-poisonous. I think that my test proved correct in this case, for it made an excellent meal.

The heat was terrific during the day and we filled the well-deck between the cockpit and hatchway with salt water, in which we kept moderately cool. Any bathing over the side is out of the question in these waters, owing to the numerous sharks and barracudas which frequent them. The supply of eggs had been replen-ished at Acapulco, and now we discovered that they were all bad and we were very pleased that this was only a short trip. On Wednesday, 13th December, we arrived at La Libertad and anchored in the open road-stead early in the morning. This added another 691 miles to our total, for which we had been at sea eight days.

La Libertad is an unprotected harbour, and though the weather was calm, a heavy swell was running from seaward. We found the *Audacious* anchored safely, and we learned from her paid hands that our two friends were in San Salvador, the capital of the country, which is about twenty-five miles from the anchorage.

On arriving in a motor-boat at the pier, we found that one was hoisted out in a truck which was lowered by a crane on the pier for the purpose. We met Mr. Towning, who acts as British Vice-Consul here in addition to his other duties. He gave us a most welcome bottle of iced beer, for it was sweltering hot ashore. He arranged for us to be driven up to San Salvador to join our friends.

The town itself was about 2,000 feet above sea-level. Coffee is the main topic of conversation here, and we were soon introduced to the owners of some large plantations. Four of our hosts had not been to bed on the previous night, but after bathing in a lake at daylight they seemed none the worse for their lack of sleep. One of them was rather frightened of being seen by his father, who was manager of an important business across the square, the building being visible from the hotel to which we had been taken. However, the father's chief attraction seemed to be the señoritas who passed his windows. His son did, however, take the precaution of leaving the hotel by the barber's shop, which opened on to a side street. We were taken to lunch at a restaurant kept by the only Japanese resident in the country. He was busy cutting open a large turtle on our arrival. Some of his attractive daughters, the result of his alliance with a Salvadorian lady, attended to our wants.

We went later to the Country Club, and on the way there we passed the golf-course, where two of our crew had been taken by the British Consul. The life at sea did not seem to have improved their game, for when we had watched one of them do three " air-shots " off the first tee, we continued on our way.

We were shown around the town that evening by our Salvadorian friends. The father of one of these owned one-third of the whole country, which is approximately the same size as Wales. It has many volcanoes, is very thickly populated, and consists mainly of coffee-plantations. One of our friends managed three of these ranches, while another six were looked after by the rest of his family. Like in Mexico, everybody of importance carries a gun, and, though there are not usually many occasions on which they are brought into play, a fortnight before our arrival an unfortunate gentleman had been the recipient of six pistol-shots from a gallant lady while telephoning in the lounge of our hotel.

One day we were taken out to one of the largest coffee-ranches in this country, where we saw the whole process of washing, shelling, sorting and drying of the beans. Nearly all the machinery for these various processes was of British manufacture and most of the finished article was shipped to Germany. When we were there, a law had recently been passed ordaining that coffee for Germany had to be shipped in German steamers. Each ranch employed about fifteen hundred labourers, who with their wide-brimmed hats and dark scowls gave one the impression of being a pretty tough crowd. Each " ranch " has a house attached to it, with a large staff of servants, so this particular family kept nine country houses going in addition to their town house.

We were keen to get to sea again as soon as possible, as we were fearing a very long passage from La Libertad to Panama, as the calms are a famous feature of that Gulf. We therefore left our American friends behind and set sail again after a short stay of only two days. The following record, kept at the time, will give an accurate picture of the joys and sorrows of sailing a small boat without an engine in these waters.

" *Friday,* 15*th December.*

" Left Larry and Arthur up there—they follow us to Panama. Bade farewell to our host and motored down to La Libertad, the car full up with provisions. Before we finally sailed, at about 4 p.m., Towning loaded us up with reading matter and gave us a very cheery send-off, blowing his steamboat's whistle furiously, which was taken up by the ss. *Salvador,* a British ship which had arrived during our absence. We did fifty-nine miles up to noon to-day—Saturday, 16th December—but we have not moved at all this afternoon. Owing to the lack of air it is very sultry, or is it the reaction after the excellent Salvadorian hospitality ? I wish there was some wind occasionally down this coast, as our letters will be at Panama.

" *Thursday,* 21*st December.*

" We have not done so badly for the first week, getting some fresh breezes which have given us the following days' runs.

" Friday,   15th December, left La Libertad at 15.30.
Saturday,   16th   ,,   59 miles.
Sunday,   17th   ,,   71 miles.
Monday,   18th   ,,   116 miles.
Tuesday,   19th   ,,   57 ,,
Wednesday, 20th   ,,   39 ,,
Thursday, 21st   ,,   17 ,,

" We started off in a wave of pessimism about the length of time that we would take to reach Panama. Now that most yachts have an engine and very few are entirely reliant on sail, one is told that there is no wind whatever in certain areas. On arrival there one usually find some breeze at intervals to help us along. That is what we are doing now, and though our progress is slow we are not failing to make some headway. The boat is comparatively cool when there is some wind, but as soon as that drops one realises how hot it is. As is always the case in the Tropics, the hour before sunrise and the hour after sunset are the best times of the day.

" On Tuesday morning we could see a liner away on the horizon, steering a southerly course. We noticed she was altering course in our direction. She proved to be a French liner, the ss. *Washington*, who passed very close to us and gave us a good chuck-up. She had on board a friend of George's and Philip's whom they had met in Salvador. We were becalmed at the time and so naturally envied them their fifteen or sixteen knots.

" Yesterday morning Larry in *Audacious* arrived, having left La Libertad on Sunday evening. He drew up close alongside and later left us for Panama. His engine seems all right again.

"We are now nearing Cape Blanco Light, which guards the entrance to the Gulf of Nicoya on the Costa Rica coast. There is little or no wind. Before starting out I prophesied for the time taken to reach Panama twenty-four days; Philip twenty-five, Bertie thirty, and Red eighteen. It will be interesting to see how long we really do take, and I hope the last proves right! It is amusing to note how our optimism soared at first, when we were getting some fresh breeze occasionally. but now we are more silent over our chances of 'seeing the New Year in' at Panama. There are plenty of fish around, but we are not making enough speed through the water to catch them; there are also plenty of sea-snakes, brown, with ringed tails, and about a couple of feet in length. We have been following the coast, thereby taking advantage of the land-and-sea breezes, which are a saving grace. The foreshore is a thick mass of mangrove bushes with ranges of high hills as a background.

"We have our beds more or less permanently on the upper deck, though usually in the afternoon there is not sufficient shade and we go down below. I have got my own bed below the fore-hatch, where, if there is any wind, I get the advantage of it and am sheltered from the heat of the sun at the same time.

"We are feeding well, though apart from a snack at mid-day, we restrict ourselves to breakfast and supper, both of which are usually 'ample' meals! I find I am growing fat, but my present excuse is that I'm getting ready for the cold of the Atlantic. Actually, for I swore on a very early page of this journal to be honest, I eat too much—and I like it!

" *Friday, 22nd December*, 9 p.m.

" At last we have got past the rock on which stands that miserable Cape Blanco lighthouse, every detail of which must be indelibly stamped on our memories. Every time we looked like approaching it, the strong current prevailing overcame what little wind there was, so this morning we found ourselves exactly where we had been twenty-four hours earlier. Our day's run up to noon was exactly two miles ! To-day has been more successful.

" At 6.30 I was awakened by excited voices, as a porpoise was firmly harpooned, our best success with that weapon. I am afraid that the prospects of dealing with his carcase met with rather an unwilling response on my part. However, this was wisely ignored by the remainder, who got her inboard despite my protests. It was lucky that we had a doctor on board who knew where the liver was situated ! I was presented with a large liver, enough steaks for thirty normal people, the heart, tongue and kidneys. Observing the keeping qualities of any flesh are impaired by the hot weather, some compromise had to be reached. We therefore had the liver for breakfast and it was really very good. The steak is now stewing for supper. Sharks soon came round when we ditched the carcase. The wind rose sufficiently to get us away from the ' bloody ' scene, past the lighthouse—the headquarters of hundreds of booby-birds—and now it is some ten miles astern, and the wind is again falling light.

" To noon to-day, Friday—two miles, making nineteen miles in two days ! !

" *Thursday, 28th December.*

" Christmas has come and gone, and now we find ourselves near Cape Mala, with about 130 miles to go to Panama. We got very much better winds finally than we had expected to experience, and once we had got clear of Cape Blanco, where, as related above, we were stationary for nearly two days, we came along quite well. Dec. 23rd, Dec. 28th, noon to noon, we have done 344 miles, a daily average of fifty-seven. This may not appear anything very wonderful, but we started off down this part of the coast with prophecies, by people with expert knowledge, of no wind at all, so we are pleased to find that we are getting the land-and-sea breezes as far as this. Now the wind is blowing fairly fresh from the northward, and we may be going to have our work cut out to get into this Gulf, owing to a current of about one to one-and-a-half knots which is not helping matters at the moment.

" Christmas Day was much the same as the others until the evening, when we allowed ourselves some California white wine with supper. After this we went on deck and got into communication with a merchant ship, the *City of Culebra*, and we had a very cheerful exchange of signals. As they disappeared in the direction of Los Angeles, they informed us that they were enjoying ' turkey with trimmings.' We did not run to that, but I do not think that there are many complaints about the food.

" The first cylinder of rock-gas has emptied to-day, so it has lasted about fifty days, and I reckon that, by leaving Panama with both cylinders full, we should have enough to take us home and meet any emergency.

We have a great deal of signalling now that we are in the shipping route, and it passes the watches well ; the steamers must wonder who the devil we are !

"We are in an area of rainstorms now which cause hurried exits from the upper deck quite often. Our fishing is a failure, except when close in to shore. We are all in splendid health, but rather flabby, while two of us are noticeably larger in circumference than when we set out. The thought of being so close to Panama makes one realise that time is getting on, and, though we naturally look forward to getting home, we are in no hurry to do so. We are all wondering what the weather will be like on the Atlantic side.

"*Monday,* 1st *January,* 1934.

"We are making our way slowly *across* the Gulf of Panama. We found by our noon position that we had a current of about one knot with us, so perhaps we shall get along quicker now. We have about one hundred and fifty miles' sailing to reach Panama.

"We are all very energetic, as, strangely enough, the weather is quite cool, due to the north-east wind, presumably. The others have been refitting ropes, tackles, etc., while I painted the galley—and myself, yesterday. The 'rib' of our collapsible boat fell down from overhead in the saloon, two days ago, and caught Bertie a good smack in the eye. Though it smashed his monocle and cut his eyelid badly, the physician seems to have healed himself most successfully.

"We caught a Coryphene last night which had been following us for some time. They have a square head, with a hard upper ridge, and are a beautiful green colour with rainbow spots. We had hooked this one in the eye, which is placed very low in this fish. Our text-book on these matters advised us that, though they were a change from salt tack, their flesh was rather coarse. This one was so alive with worms that one would have had to have been very coarse oneself to have eaten it with any relish, so we threw him overboard again. It is very annoying, as our fresh food is getting very low ; we have finished the potatoes and now we are nearly out of onions and eggs.

" We had a little wine again for supper, to float the New Year in.

" Average for the last four days—twenty-seven miles.

" *Tuesday, 2nd January.*

" Not a breath of wind all day, so it is baking hot. However, current is definitely setting us in northerly direction parallel to the coast of Ecuador. Cordilleras de Los Andes in sight. Optimism prevails again ; we should reach Panama within a week, as we have only about one hundred and twenty miles more to do. To noon to-day we did thirty miles.

" *Wednesday, 3rd January.*

" Again very little wind, but with a favourable current we had done another forty-five miles up to noon to-day.

" Supper last night was disturbed by a most amusing incident. Bertie stole down to the saloon, motioned to us to make as little noise as possible, and announced that he could distinctly hear the quacking of duck, and even asserted that he could just distinguish their forms close at hand. Philip crept up to the top of the ladder with the gun, and giving vent to our excitement in hushed whispers, the rest of us followed. Sure enough we could see their plump bodies. Philip pointed the gun and we switched on the Aldis lamp and, with our hands to our ears, waited for the bang. It never came, for, sitting on a floating baulk of timber were six or seven 'boobies,' who were obviously a bit dazed at this nocturnal interference with their slumbers, and with the row of white breasts illuminated by our lamp presented a most comic appearance.

"To-night we all trooped on deck again, as there was a small vessel on our starboard bow, and the helmsman assured us that she had been signalling. We got the Aldis on to her and over she came. Her highly indignant queries, first in Spanish and then in English, as to what we wanted, remained unanswered, I'm afraid. She was a motor fishing-vessel, and the light was a swinging stern light.

"It is amusing to note that for supper this evening we had some very thick lentil soup, with suet jam-roll to follow. Not bad for this part of the world ! We are frightfully pleased with the progress and the possible chance of getting in to-morrow, as we have only fifty miles to go.

"9 p.m., *Thursday, 4th January*.

"As good as in—six miles to go to the Quarantine Anchorage, and quite a good breeze. Up to noon to-day, another thirty-eight miles.

"This current certainly has been a blessing. There is a story of a sailing-ship which got becalmed in the centre of Panama Bay on the edge of the currents. She drifted helplessly around the centre of the bay, and finally, when a thick growth of weeds had attached themselves to her bottom, she had to be abandoned !

"We have been very busy again to-day—refitting ropes, etc., and painting out down below. We are all very excited at the thought of getting our letters to-morrow. The weather has been very hot during the last few days, but cools off at night. We finished the eggs and the onions to-day.

"*Stop Press*. Anchored at twenty minutes after midnight."

So the crossing of the Pacific Ocean, with its varying weather, was an accomplished fact, and this the last leg of it had proved the most trying of the lot ; the last 855 miles from La Libertad to Panama had taken us twenty and a half days, giving a daily average of only 41·6 miles.

CHAPTER XV

Through the Panama Canal and into the Atlantic

On arrival at Balboa, which is the port at the Pacific end of the Panama Canal, we found that the American Navy were on the look-out for us. They towed us to a berth alongside a battle-practice target. We found the *Audacious* here, with her crew on board, but our two friends had temporarily returned by 'plane to the States. We collected our mail, which had reached welcome proportions by that time.

One of our first steps was to call on the American Admiral. In answer to our expression of thanks for his assistance, he told us of an amusing experience that he had had. As a young man, he was serving in a squadron which visited Hong-Kong. For a whole week they were right royally entertained. On the last evening of all a hectic farewell party was drawing to a close, and they were expressing their gratitude to their British hosts. A young British officer, who had himself taken full advantage of the evening to enjoy himself, cut short at once with, "Quite all right, fellows, quite all right; we had ORDERS, you see!" Whether history had again repeated itself or not I do not know, but we found a most hospitable welcome from the American Navy at all these places.

We were keen to transit the canal as soon as possible, but having no engine it looked as if this was going to mean hiring a tug, which would have been extremely expensive. During our short stay there, the British Minister, Sir Josiah Crosby, Captain Payne, O.B.E., and others gave us a fine welcome, and we were most grateful when through their kind offices arrangements were made for an interview with the Governor of Panama. He in turn very kindly allowed us to be towed through free of charge, and as there was a load of bananas to go through, it was arranged that *Tai-Mo-Shan* should be secured alongside the diesel lighter which was transporting them.

Balboa would be unbearably hot were it not for the daily shower of rain which keeps the place at a moderate temperature. The gardens and grass lawns which surround the houses in the canal zone are a refreshing sight.

Lying close to us was the *Svaap*, a small ketch in which her owner had sailed for over three years, doing 32,000 miles. As we had all read of his adventures in his book, we were glad to meet Robinson. He had got married, and now his wife was helping him get the vessel ready for further wanderings. They had just had bad luck through the stupidity of a native river-pilot who had anchored them for the night in what he chose as the best spot. In the morning the tide had gone down and left some tree-stumps sticking up through the bottom of the *Svaap*. The canal zone seems to be a clearing-house for men who have been overcome by *wanderlust*. A small sailing-vessel was at anchor here which closely resembled a British steam pinnace, and flew the Red Ensign. Sure enough that is what she was, and as she had been built at Glasgow, in 1906, she spoke well for British labour. The captain of the *Red-Riding-Hood*,

i

for such was her name, was an interesting character. He had lost an eye from the hang-fire of a six-inch gun when as breech-worker he was serving in the American Navy. He now styled himself Captain and conchologist, and spent his life collecting coral, shells, sponges and other marine curiosities, which have such a prolific growth in these waters.

The treasure-hunters on their way to Cocos Island pass through here, and a British party did so while we were there. The lure of hidden treasure at Cocos Island is nothing new. Some years ago two old ladies got hold of a man who, they thought, would suit their purpose, and unfolded their plan to him. They would charter a ship, which he was to take out from England around the Horn (it was before the days of the Panama Canal), and then he was to meet them at the Pacific end of the Isthmus and take them to Cocos Island. I met this man, and he told me how he had carried out his instructions, and how the old ladies, having travelled out in a more comfortable liner, had turned up at the appointed rendezvous. They were armed with a map, as all good treasure-hunters should be, but failed to find the treasure. This man was still convinced of its existence on Cocos Island, and did all in his power to persuade us to visit there and discover it. However attractive it might have sounded, we had our voyage to complete and were unable to join the enthusiasts who still do believe in it.

On the morning of Tuesday, 8th January, we had breakfast at a very early hour aboard the American minesweeper, *Teal*. We then awaited the arrival of the diesel lighter with its cargo of bananas. On her arrival

we secured *Tai-Mo-Shan* alongside, and from then on-
wards we did not have to worry about steering her.
We got a great thrill out of our passage through the
Panama Canal. We went through the Miraflores Lock
astern of the ss. *Brainton* of Newcastle. She had left
Vancouver on the 23rd of December, while we had
sailed out of those straits on the 27th of September.
All the coloured hands at the locks got quite excited
when they discovered our nationality, as they are
British subjects from the West Indies, and are very proud
of the fact. We had none of the troubles which other
small boats have had in the locks due to the swishing
of the waters, as the fact of being made fast alongside
the lighter prevented all worry. The remarkable effi-
ciency of the working of the locks and the electric loco-
motives filled us with admiration. At Gatun we were
walking along the lock wall when a policeman hurried
up and demanded to know from what ship we had
broken out. He joined in the merriment when we
pointed out *Tai-Mo-Shan*, who was all but hidden by
the pile of bananas.

As soon as we arrived at the Cristobal end of the coast
we were met by a U.S. Navy launch, and taken straight
to the Fleet Air Base at Coco Solo. The eight days that
we spent here as guests of the American flying officers
were under most comfortable conditions. Their base
was a grand place, with every form of entertainment
for the men, such as swimming-baths, cinemas, can-
teens, and so forth. When they saw *Tai-Mo-Shan* by
daylight they insisted on getting busy on her. She was
a much smarter-looking craft when we nosed our way
into the waters of the Atlantic on 17th January.

Our introduction to this ocean was of a different nature to the calm weather which we had been so recently experiencing down the Pacific coast. In fact, so ominous was the line of spray which hid the breakwater from view that I have to admit that I rushed up to Panama by motor-car shortly before the time arranged for the start. Once we were at sea and heading into big seas, my bearing became almost haughty. My four companions realised that I had cheated the elements by purchasing an anti-seasick remedy, but perhaps I had some excuse, observing that meals were always demanded, whatever the weather. We certainly never missed one. I mention this question of sea-sickness because it is undoubtedly a big deterrent to those who might otherwise enjoy an ocean cruise. Before starting on this trip I had secret qualms about my ability to stick it out. I thought of the days aboard a certain destroyer off Cape Wrath, the well-named promontory forming the north-west point of Scotland ; and many other occasions on board various types of warships. I remembered stories I had read by other ocean-voyagers where men had been so seasick that the skipper had dosed them liberally with salt water, and I had kept my fears to myself and had set off from Hong-Kong, only to be violently ill as soon as we were clear of the harbour. There was no alternative but to hope for the best, and invariably I found that after the first day or two, which admittedly was rather misery, I could afford to scoff at the sea, the wind and the motion of the boat. Though I managed to eat my meals somehow during these bad periods, I never managed to attain perfection, like one of our sick members did, by returning to the saloon and

F

devouring a second meal in place of the one which he had just lost.

As soon as we were clear of the breakwater, Captain Molten, the Commanding Officer of the Fleet Air Base, came out in a 'plane and took photographs of us from every angle. We got these on arrival in England, and they show the vessel under rough weather conditions, a view which we had always wanted to obtain throughout our cruise and which we ourselves were naturally unable to do.

The wind was from the north-east, which was not in our favour, and necessitated sailing close-hauled, our approximate courses being E. and N. by W. However, we were battling along nobly, though the bumpy, short motion was rather trying at first. To start with, we worked along the South American shore, our next goal being Jamaica, which necessitated crossing the Caribbean Sea. As a glance at the map will show you, Cartagena, to which we worked our way, is on the coast of Colombia across the Gulf of Darien. We wanted to make for Kingston, Jamaica, on one tack. We experienced a westerly set of about thirty-three miles daily, which did not help matters, but apart from some short tacks to avoid Portland Rock at the eastern end of Pedro Bank, we achieved our object. When we anchored in the quarantine anchorage at Port Royal, after eight days' sailing, we were well pleased with the performance of the boat, as we had sailed 755 miles to windward at a daily average of ninety miles. In fact, for three days of this windward work we did 369 miles. We were better pleased to be in harbour on this occasion than after considerably longer periods at sea during the calm weather, as the motion made eating, cooking and sleeping much harder problems.

On the morning of Friday, the 26th of January, we were eager to make our way up harbour, as we could see the masts and funnels of a British cruiser. Unfortunately the wind had completely dropped, leaving us drifting helplessly between the buoys which marked the entrance to the channel. We lay there, cursing our ill-fortune, when another cruiser approached the entrance from seaward. We assembled our collapsible boat as quickly as we could and, lowering it over the side, attempted to tow our bow clear of the channel entrance. This was the first English warship that we had sighted since we had left Chinese waters, seven months before. She passed close to us, and we soon saw that it was H.M.S. *Dragon*, one of the cruisers on the West Indies station. She summoned aid, and we were towed up harbour and secured alongside the wharf close to H.M.S. *Danae*, another cruiser of the same squadron.

From the moment that we arrived until the time came for us to be on our way again we were given a magnificent time. We had met many friends aboard H.M.S. *Danae*, while Sir Ransford and Lady Slater at Government House made us very welcome. The beauties of Jamaica are too well known to need description here. Apart from bathing-picnics under ideal conditions, dances and other entertainments of a like nature, we inspected a banana plantation and the arrangements for sinking wells for irrigation purposes. We also saw a sugar and rum factory, and were presented with an ample allowance of the latter commodity with which to stock our vessel. The banana crops, the sugar-canes, the coffee and the citrus fruits depend for their existence on the absence of hurricanes, which do such terrible damage in a short time. Native divers scraped our bottom clean for a few shillings.

We left Jamaica on 3rd February, with a great case of oranges, grape-fruit, sweet potatoes, yams, cho-cho's, etc., and planned to visit the Bahamas on our way to Bermuda.

The following record, kept at the time, will best describe the adventures which were to befall us after a fine send-off from our many friends in Jamaica :

" *Tuesday, 6th February.*

" Am writing this under rather ' upsetting ' conditions, so writing will suffer in consequence. We are in the middle of ' Windward Passage,' which separates Cuba and Haiti. We had east winds to start with, which suited us, but recently the wind has backed to north-east, and we are experiencing a good deal of rain. The internal comfort is suffering considerably. Every available garment soon seems to be damp—if not actually wet. However, we are far from being miserable, as the temperature, though it has now dropped to seventy-eight degrees at noon, is not yet sufficiently low to make clothes a very important matter.

" At the moment we are steering for Little Inagua Island, where we are hoping to do some surveying and visit other small islands in the vicinity as well. The wind is force 3 from the N.E., and our course North. The sea is ' lumpy ' and we have about 160 miles direct to reach this small island. My mattress, which is filled with kapok, and usually very comfortable, gives me a very hard 'ride' in this motion. I really must refold all the old clothes which I have bundled underneath it from time to time for the sake of a better stowage. Everything is beginning to smell musty. 'Red' goes on getting sights in an almost miraculous manner. We are all getting on well and eating heartily, which is synonymous with good cheer.

"I heard an amusing story from H.M.S. *Danae*.—When they were at Miami recently, the officers decided to give a small dance. At the foot of the invitation-cards was printed 'R.S.V.P.—Small Dance.' The Mess Secretary was a little surprised when he was handed a reply which began : 'Dear Mr. Small Dance—'

"Here are details of progress :

"Feb. 2nd at 1430. Cast off from Kingston, Jamaica. Cheered *Danae*.

To Noon.

Sat.	3rd Feb.	48 miles	17° 29′ N.	76° 05′ W.
			(Wind E.-N.E., force 3)	
Sun.	4th ,,	54 ,,	17° 25′ N.	75° 09′ W.
			(Wind E.-N.E., force 3)	
Mon.	5th ,,	48 ,,	18° 02′ N.	74° 36′ W.
			(heavy rain all day.)	
Tues.	6th ,,	70 ,,	19° 11′ N.	74° 20′ W.
Wed.	7th ,,	78 ,,	20° 26′ N.	74° 00′ W.
Thurs.	8th ,,	54 ,,	21° 17′ N.	73° 41′ W.
Fri.	9th ,,	40 ,,	—1000.	

Hove-to off island of Little Inagua, and later anchored inside reef.

Though we have been expecting a 'Norther' (which is the term by which the local gales are known) for some days, we have actually been enjoying wonderful weather, with an easterly wind averaging force 2.

On Thursday we beat up past Great Inagua, which we passed close enough to see the low green scrub with occasional palm-trees and long sandy beaches. These islands look more attractive from seaward than is usually the case when you land on them.

" Yesterday morning (Friday) found us in the vicinity of Little Inagua, and so excited were we all at the prospect of exploring it that we had breakfast very punctually and waited about impatiently for some time afterwards. You see, the only information that we had was in the Pilot Manual for these waters, which was as follows :

" ' *Little Inagua Island* is somewhat quadrangular in form ; eight miles in length in an East and West direction, and about five miles in breadth ; in the centre of the island is a flat hill sixty feet high. . . .

" ' *Water*. There are no inhabitants, but wild hogs are said to exist on the island, and consequently there must be water.'

" When we got to the vicinity of the reef which sheltered the only anchorage on the southern shore, we lowered the dinghy, into which Philip and I clambered. We took with us a lead-and-line and a buoy for marking the entrance. We pulled about, taking soundings across the gap in the reef, and finally dropped our buoy to mark the termination of the reef to windward. We then signalled *Tai-Mo-Shan* to advance, and with Red keeping a look-out aloft she came whistling around the buoy and anchored inside the reef. The light-green water was mottled with streaks of mahogany-brown which betrayed the presence of rocks. We sounded close to our anchorage and finally decided that the position was too unhealthy to allow us to remain there. We also decided that a survey, unless of a very complete and accurate character, would not serve any more useful purpose than a good description of the anchorage would do. However, seeing a wreck lying on the sandy shore, we decided to investigate it before leaving, while the thought of hunting wild hog was a most attractive one.

" I have never seen the boat lying in a more beautiful setting than she appeared to us from ashore. As a background were the white wave-tops dispersing in a smother of foam as they crashed on the reef's outer edge ; inside the reef the water was a beautiful light-green with which the hull of *Tai-Mo-Shan* blended admirably. Occasionally a cruel, jagged set of coral fingers protruded from the water, while the wavelets wasted their energy against them, leaving behind a small area of bubbling spume. Closer inshore the more plentiful streaks of brown reminded one of the presence of innumerable dangers.

" We went in in our boat, and luckily got ashore without tearing the canvas hull. There was a long sandy beach, but running down close to it was thick scrub. We examined the beach and were surprised to find footprints and, later on, a pile of conch shells and remnants of a temporary shelter. These were evidently the remains of fishermen from Great Inagua. Though we saw no wild hog, we learned later that there were wild jackass on the island. George and Philip went with me to the top of the highest eminence, which was actually about the same height as our mast. What a walk we had, as we were in shorts, and the scrub served as a covering to numerous cactus-bushes. The latter were of all shapes and sizes—squat round ones, tall thin ones, some with flowers, some without, but all possessed of very sharp prickles, which they managed to plant some inches into our flesh at every step we took. The ground was like a large expanse of ‘ crazy pavement,’ except where an occasional deep hole reminded us of its volcanic origin. There was certainly no place for any habitation, and the few birds that we saw were so tame that it was obvious that man’s real nature had not been revealed to them. The wreck was evidently that of a fisherman’s boat, and our dreams of doubloons and similar hidden treasure were not realised this time !

“ We sailed at 4 p.m., and decided to make for Crooked Island to make a further exploration there.

“ *Sunday, 11th February.*

“ Had a rather miserable, squally night, which made it unpleasant on deck, and turned sleep into a series of bad dreams below. I find that the latter is constantly the case with me when being tossed about in the bunk.

“ Early this morning a low fringe of yellow sands denoted the presence of Crooked Island. At one end the lighthouse showed up a dazzling white against the bright blue of the sky behind it. We navigated with great caution, sounding frequently with the lead, while Ryder directed operations from aloft. A small boat rowed by a couple of black natives directed us to an anchorage in the bay, which is sheltered by the island from the prevailing winds. We dropped our anchor outside the reef, and waited for the first arrivals.

“ Our visitors to date have all been of the McKinney family—Jeulius Stafford, the father, and James Arthur and Stafford Alaxander, the sons (their spelling, not mine). The others have gone ashore, but I remained behind to square up stores, write up this diary, etc. I seem to have persuaded the McKinney family that work is excellent for them. Jeulius is working on the sails, James Arthur is cleaning some ' market ' fish, which he has just caught for me, while Stafford Alaxander is scrubbing the deck. They all address me as ' Cookie.' This causes me a good deal of amusement ; I wonder what they would say if I turned up here in full dress !

" This is a quaint little place. I gather from Stafford Alaxander that a few years ago they grew a quantity of fruit, and several ships loaded with oranges here. A hurricane, followed by a tidal wave, seems to have destroyed that, about two years ago. My questions about the latter produced a long story, going into most gruesome details of how the cemetery was washed away. However, they went round the mangrove trees, getting the boxes down and reburied them. He tells me that they were collecting bones for some weeks. ' Terrible, terrible,' he ended. Though he has never really counted them, he reckons that there must be one hundred inhabitants in this settlement. One of the latter sent me off a pumpkin, with the request that I would ' trade ' him a little tea and cheese. This I have done. I have just sent my washing ashore, and apparently I am supposed to produce a little sugar as payment. I am looking forward to the return of the others, to hear the news. This is an open anchorage, and it is blowing hard a little further to seaward, but here we have sufficient lee to lie quite comfortably.

"*Monday, 12th February.*

"It is 9.25 p.m. and the boat is moving slightly to a swell which has been left behind by a southerly wind that has been blowing throughout the day. It was nearly the cause of our getting under way and leaving rather hurriedly, but luckily it died down with sunset, and made it unnecessary to do so. A duck-flighting party had been fixed for the early hours of this morning, but as the locals responsible for the organisation were afraid of calling us, it luckily fell through ! We all breakfasted decently at about half-past eight !

"When the others came off last night we had a very cosy party. Really, these small places are much the most enjoyable. We had an excellent supper of ' market ' fish, just freshly caught, sweet potatoes, yams, and last, but by no means least, Jamaica rum. We had such a friendly feeling one towards the other by dealing with these victuals that we were able to come to some quick decisions, one being that Dartmouth is to be our final goal. Our date of arrival there we plan to be about the first of April, and we can let our friends know from Bermuda without publishing it abroad. We also discussed the question of writing a book, and decided to do so.

"To-day started off by the arrival of Arthur and his father, and one John Gibson, who had brought a cray-fish as an offering. After the usual salutations of ' Good morning, Captain, good morning, Cookie,' etc. we had a bathe and breakfast. I landed with Arthur afterwards, being preceded by Bertie and George. When we got ashore we trudged along the beach and I was shown where the cemetery had existed before the tidal wave of two years ago. The only visible remains were dark patches in the ground for which the most morbid explanations were forthcoming—but enough. A little further on was a pile of loose stones covering quite a large area, in the corner of which was a small lump of masonry. It was explained to me that the latter was all that remained of a store kept by a man and his wife for fifty years. Apparently, so loath were they to leave, after so long a period, that the old lady (presumably she must have been) was drowned and carried some three hundred yards inland, while her husband also followed in her footsteps a week later. I was shown their graves too.

"A heap of rocks was pointed out to me as the English church, while yet another, close by, apparently represented what had once been a school-house. This brought me, with my escort, to the door of a stout-looking dwelling. Here I was introduced to Grandpa, a chronic invalid who could talk of little but his maladies, his wife, the present schoolmistress, and others, of what relationship one to another I am none too clear. Of one thing, however, I was not left long in doubt, and that was that they were all eager, for obvious reasons, to meet the man who had charge of the provisions. The old man had quite a sense of humour on those rare occasions when he was not discussing his ailments, and told me how he had sent off a pumpkin yesterday, with a request for some cheese, but he could not see the latter when they brought it to him ! However, we all laughed heartily, and he decided that he now wanted tea, sugar and a host of other things. This seemed a little one-sided until I got all his fowls mustered and chose my bird, which, suitably denuded, etc., is to appear on board to-morrow.

" Further along the village I came across a sight which I shall always remember. Outside a small, white-walled house with two rooms were some fifteen or twenty men, women and infants. Some were exhibiting their recently-extracted molars to those on the waiting-list, who wore rather apprehensive expressions while they covered their cheek with a hand or the end of a shawl. I entered the first room, and there I found George. He had all the patients well in hand and, having personally examined their mouths, was all ready for the next case for the inner room. In the latter Bertie was having a strenuous time, especially as some of them were in a really bad way.

" I felt that I was not wanted, but, stopping for a moment outside, I was informed by the patients that God must have sent him.

" Arthur and I then went on our way to shoot duck. It was extremely hot, and by the time that we had done four miles, mostly through thick and prickly bush, I felt exhausted. I swam out to the middle of a small lake to retrieve two small divers which I had shot. We visited several other pools without adding to the bag.

" On the chart there is a spot here called ' Marine Farm.' I think that it is quite reasonable to have thought that this would indicate some sort of fish-pond. Well, I went there. It meant going to the top of a small rise over loose stone and rock, through patches of Indian corn, low scrub and cactus-bushes. At the top were three or four stone buildings, of which only the walls were left standing. They were obviously the living quarters of the Marines, for this is what the 'Farm' turned out to be. Lying in thick undergrowth were three cannon. Their history would be interesting, as they were presumably landed from some ship, but it must have entailed a great deal of labour to get them into position. I took a note of the markings, as I hope to find out how they got there.

"We all had supper aboard to-night, as soon as our friends had departed with packets of sugar, flour, tea, rice, etc. Their genuine poverty is terrible, especially when one remembers that before this hurricane and tidal wave, fruit, coconuts and vegetables were plentiful. Pop McKinney is to call us at five-thirty to-morrow for duck-shooting, so I must follow the example of the others and get to bed."

CHAPTER XVI

Ashore on Crooked Island in the Bahamas

The diary continues as follows :

" Little could I have believed it, should anyone have suggested to me when writing the above, that the continuation thereof would be under the conditions in which I now find myself. It is about 10 a.m. and I am lying on the sand, with a sail for a tent, while similar erections form quite a sizable camp around me. Twenty yards away the incoming tide is swishing up under the stern of *Tai-Mo-Shan*. She is lying on firm sand on her port side, listed over some forty to forty-five degrees, and is undamaged—or that is my firm belief. I think that there is scarcely any necessity for me to record our feelings, though we have all managed to face the situation cheerfully, I think. I must try to remember and set down in an orderly manner the events which have happened and the steps we have taken to get her off since Tuesday morning.

" Luckily Bertie has scribbled some notes and, helped by these, I can piece these activities together :

" *Monday, 12th February.*

" I turned in after writing this diary, the remainder already having done so ; Red was sleeping on deck. Throughout the day the wind had been veering steadily and, taken in conjunction with the weather maps, westerly winds were indicated. When I got on board just before dark, Red was considering shifting billet, and had it not been for the fact that we had laundry and stores still ashore, which the natives declined to bring on board after dark, we would have gone to sea there and then. However, in view of these things being still ashore and the wind falling, we remained at anchor. By half-past seven there was only a gentle breeze blowing, and everything seemed satisfactory.

" At about midnight we all got a call, and hurried on deck. The wind had freshened from the west, which gave us a ' lee ' shore, so we set the mainsail and commenced to weigh anchor. The latter operation is necessarily a slow one, and while we were still at ' short stay ' we grounded lightly. After a couple of light tremors we seemed to be clear, and sailed away on the starboard tack. The anchor was now aweigh, and though they were anxious moments, we did not then think the position desperate. It was a dark night, and we could not judge our distance from the shore accurately, but it was obviously close enough at hand to make ' going about ' a necessity. This we proceeded to do, having plenty of way on the boat for the purpose. As she righted herself, however, prior to ' paying-off ' on the opposite tack, the keel touched bottom, owing to the increased draught. Three times we went through this agonising manœuvre, which we attempted to bring about successfully with the aid of a long bamboo-pole, but unfortunately in vain. It was then that we became stranded.

" We have always had an orderly organisation for stowing things, and it now served us in good stead, for we had the boat assembled and in the water in next to no time. George and I got into it and, taking the kedge-anchor from the starboard bow, proceeded to lay it out on that quarter. If it had only held, it would have saved the situation. As soon as it was obvious that the kedge was ' coming home,' Bertie and Philip attempted to take out one of our heavy anchors slung under the boat, but despite furious effort on their part this proved impossible to accomplish.

" A fresh sea was breaking around us by this time. At about a quarter-past one in the morning I swam ashore and, stumbling about the beach, I made my way to the settlement. I estimate the boat to have been about seventy-five yards from the shore when I left.

" There was little to be done on board in the meanwhile ; the list was about forty degrees and she was bumping, while, to make matters worse, the wind was freshening. I had to curb my impatience while the first man that I awakened went to tell his next-door neighbour, and so on throughout the community. It was about 4 a.m. when I got back to *Tai-Mo-Shan*, who by this time had drifted into shallow water, where she lay over on her port side, parallel to the shore.

" *Tuesday,* 13th *February.*

" The weather now made boatwork impossible, so it was decided that it was imperative to place her in the best position relative to the seas, to prevent damage. High water was at daybreak, so we took the heavy anchor ashore and the heaviest ropes at our disposal ; these consisted of the kedge-anchor and sea-anchor warps. With each lift of the vessel we hauled her a little further up the beach. The manœuvre was greatly hindered by the difficulty of getting anything to which we could make fast our anchors on shore. We even buried the ' spinnaker ' booms in the sand, but these dragged through the sand as soon as the weight of the boat came on them. Finally we secured our anchors round the stems of the largest trees, which were small palms—' palmettos,' as they are known in these parts. They bore the strain moderately well.

" The seas swished under the stern of the vessel, and though she lifted gently, we were delighted to find that during the forenoon the motion was certainly not sufficient to cause any serious damage. The vessel had listed over on her port side, at an angle of fifty or sixty degrees. We decided to unload her, to minimise the strain. The angle at which the boat was lying did not make this easy, and in an atmosphere of intense depression and suppressed excitement we started to empty out the contents of the vessel. We thought of those weeks of preparation which we had spent at Hong-Kong before the start in fitting everything into place. In a little under two hours we had completely emptied the interior of the boat of everything movable. Tins of provisions, wireless and navigation instruments, coils of wire and rope, bundles of clothes, sails and books followed each other up the ladder in quick succession, and were passed from hand to hand by the natives, who stretched up the beach to the spot where we had decided to make our camp.

" The tiller broke on several occasions, despite the heavy lashings with which we had secured it, but two of our iron reefing spanners finally held until the rudder silted up conveniently in the sand. Later on, we secured planks and with these lashed the rudder amidships, and thus prevented it from being jolted and jarred by the seas.

" Owing to the extreme poverty of the natives, little help, other than plenty of manual labour, could be expected from them. By evening we had got some sort of order ashore, and though we were badly burned by the sun throughout the day, it became comparatively cold soon after sunset. We all enjoyed the stew that night, and as soon as the last of the locals had left us we improvised shelters with the sails, and lay down to sleep.

" *Wednesday, 14th February.*

" Camp astir at an early hour. All five complained of the cold during the night, and decided on the erection of better tents when time allowed, though energies had to be directed solely on the salvage question at that stage. We had a good breakfast, as, having all our provisions ashore, we could have been in a much more unenviable position than that in which we did actually find ourselves. As soon as the meal had put new life into us, Philip went off with McKinney to the lighthouse, which was reported to have shovels and similar articles for our purpose. The weather had moderated considerably, and optimism prevailed.

" We rigged a three-fold purchase, using the mainsheet blocks and the spares, and Red, George and Bertie worked like Trojans getting ropes, tackles, wires and all the other paraphernalia with which we were to start on the all-important business of getting our vessel afloat again. I took on the job of placing the anchors. The strange thing was that, owing to the disinclination of the natives to do so, I found that I had to do nearly all the under-water work myself. We all got badly sunburned and our lips were blistered from the combined action of the sun and salt water.

"By working together in this manner we got our small anchor of 150 lbs. laid out, backed up by the larger one, 120 lbs, with a three-inch hemp strop between them. The four-inch sea-anchor warp was laid from the nearest anchor and bent on to two parts of our two and a half inch kedge-warp. After the latter had been led over the stern it was fastened to the moving block of our three-fold purchase with a stopper. A stopper on the mizzen served to hang the hauling-rope during the overhauling of the purchase.

"Now that we had rigged the gear for hauling the boat off stern first, it was obviously an added advantage if the sand could be dug away from around the stern. We had no shovels of our own, and asked the natives to procure some from the village. After a long wait a lad arrived back with one shovel. We asked for more, but had to get on as best we could with this one, as we were told that it was the only one available. We were about to set to with a will when one of the head natives stopped us. He explained that the shovel had been fetched without his consent, and that we could not use it. We were getting desperately impatient, as it was necessary to carry out the digging while the low tide enabled us to do so. In vain we pleaded with him. We were told that it was a 'Company' shovel and he was afraid that we could not use it without the permission of the chairman, who was then absent. Even our offers to purchase the shovel did not avail to alter the situation.

" Finally we got a clearer explanation on the ' Company's ' shovel situation, for it turned out that this shovel was the only one in the settlement, and they could not therefore allow it to be used in salt water, lest it endanger its principal function of burying the dead ! This was all most irritating at the time, of course, though the timely return of Philip with planks and a few shovels from the lighthouse helped to allay our real feelings.

" By 4.15 p.m. the entire village were waiting to haul, as we had summoned them with promises of a shilling a head. Their efforts, however, resulted in the parting of the sea-anchor warp, and fresh efforts were made to haul her off. This time the kedge-warp parted.

" It was now so late that there was nothing to do but to abandon operations for the evening. George then lined up our helpers and paid out twenty-five shillings to the adults, at the rate of a bob-a-nob, and two shillings and fourpence to the ' under-twelves,' at the rate of fourpence each. Meanwhile, Arthur McKinney, upon whom the guardianship of our stores had devolved, had copied the stew of the night before step by step, and so we found it all ready for us. This was a great blessing, as by this time we were both wet and despondent. The food had its usual exhilarating effect, and as we sat around the camp fire we discussed plans for shifting her, which we determined to achieve at all costs.

" Some of the proposals which I recall now were as follows : To build a breakwater around the stern of the vessel ; to hire the necessary gear from Nassau ; to hire more labour from the other settlements inland ; to attempt the hauling-off of the boat by the bow, and even to build a canal right around the area and to flood it later, and get her water-borne. Even at low tide she is never quite dry, which has greatly hindered digging operations, more especially around the stern. We dragged our very weary bodies off to bed. George and Philip rigged a tent—Bertie joined me alongside the fire. I slept like a log, but we all found it bitterly cold.

" *Thursday*, 15*th February*.

" On the morning tide we again renewed our efforts, with the help of the villagers, whose assistance was contracted for at the same rates as on the previous day. Meanwhile we have a permanent staff, consisting of a dozen of the leading locals, who are paid at the higher rate of three shillings a day. The local constable, who does not usually wear uniform, had now entered into a contract with us also, as we found this cheaper than the usual rather rapid disappearance of stores. He now blossomed forth in a peaked cap and carried a truncheon, though the rest of his clothes remained as before. He is quite a big noise, as he possesses the one and only horse in the settlement.

" Bertie, meanwhile, had set to on his own account trying to drive in a variety of wedges between the mizzen boom and the stem of the vessel, and meanwhile everyone watched furtively for any indication of movement on the part of the boat. This time the sea-anchor warp parted and, having spliced it, renewed efforts were being made, when a large steam-yacht was sighted.

" Red wasted no time in getting into a small boat and hurrying out to intercept her. We also hoisted the ensign and a signal requesting her for assistance. Red went aboard. She proved to be the *Vagabondia*, belonging to Mr. William Mellon, a relative of the late Ambassador to Great Britain. At about 11 a.m., in came two large motor-boats, various helpers from the yacht, a four-fold purchase and a seven-inch rope. Bertie had got twelve more shovels from the lighthouse, so everybody proceeded to dig vigorously. Meanwhile I again placed the anchors, but the holding-ground proved very bad. I went off for lunch to the *Vagabondia*, and while I rather impatiently sat back amidst every luxury, the others erected tents and got everything ready for the evening's attempt, when sailors were expected to assist.

" Optimism was at its height all this time. As the *Vagabondia* had communicated with Nassau, details were being asked for from there, and so we sent several signals saying that, though the vessel was aground, we hoped to refloat her. We also added that, should we require help, we would signal later, when the evening's attempt had failed—should it do so ! Unfortunately, Mr. Mellon could only prolong his stay until the next morning. As we were using his wireless as the sole means of communication, this made it imperative to ask for help if the evening attempt failed. They kindly sent some twenty-five sailors who, with the villagers, would undoubtedly have been extremely effective, had the anchors not dragged. At about 9 p.m. the sailors had to go back, taking with them a signal saying that assistance would be welcome, and supplying the necessary technical details. They sailed early the following morning.

" *Friday, 16th February.*

" A native named Ben Gibson and I determined to get these anchors to hold somehow. When we went out to examine them, we found that our nearest anchor was pretty badly bent. However, another rusty but larger anchor was obtained from the lighthouse. We put the seven-inch rope, left behind by the *Vagabondia*, out to our large anchor, dispensing with the smaller, bent anchor. We got this anchor well bedded-in, which entailed repeated diving.

" Owing to the clear waters around these islands, all native boats carry ' water-glasses.' These consist of a square of wood, two or three feet high, open at the top end but having a thick pane of glass inserted in the lower end. By putting this lower end a short way below the surface of the sea, a perfect view can be obtained of the ocean bed. Beautiful effects are created by the brightly-coloured fish, coral and shells for which these seas are famed. These water-glasses are a great help in seeing what you are doing, when you are on the surface, but I must own that I found that hauling anchors about, shackling on cable, etc., at twelve or thirteen feet, soon got very tiring. We took the lighthouse anchor out as far as the cable belonging to it would allow, having shackled it on to our first anchor. Here our rather fatiguing efforts were rewarded by a very humorous incident.

" The man who had the anchor in his boat was most anxious to prevent any damage to his craft when we turned it over the gunwale to let it go. Imagine there-fore our consternation when, after repeated warnings, off went the anchor with a splash, taking down with it Uncle John's boat. He is a funny little man at the best of times, with a bristling moustache, the like of which I have yet to see. He was cursing furiously, even before we could drag him aboard our boat, and swore at each one of us in turn with such a vehemence of language as to leave us speechless. It appeared in his mind that we were just a set of —— fools to leave the flukes of the anchor foul of his gunwale. Then somebody, to escape the volume of his wrath, took a water-glass and looked down into the depths. There could be seen the anchor, on the bottom, while the boat floated clear of it some few feet below the surface. A lashing joined the shank of the anchor to one of the thwarts of the boat ! ' Oh, yes,' (he really said a bit more) ' I remember now that I lashed it this morning when bringing it from the light-house, and I forgot all about it.' It meant more diving for us, but it was well worth all the laughter that followed at Uncle John's expense ! He joined in too, being a wonderfully good-natured native, and all along he was very optimistic about our chances of refloating the vessel.

" We had had to give up the idea of trying the morning tide, as it was pouring with rain and most of the villagers are female. As the anchors were so firmly held and the others had replaced any tackle which showed the slightest signs of weakness, my optimism was great. You can imagine how upset we all felt when long after dark we had to give up again, owing to the anchors coming home ! We went to bed very soon after supper, feeling that our best attempt had proved a failure.

" *Saturday, 17th February.*

" This journal is now up to date, and while the others have been replacing gear this morning, I have busied myself on this before the sequence of events is forgotten. I am relieved to find that the anchors had not dragged ;

the shank has parted in two, which is nobody's fault. We are now left with a rather bent one, and have not yet found the kedge-anchor, which we left further out on our first evening. We are expecting a ship called the *Firebird* to be sent to our assistance. Hauling us off should not prove very difficult. All is rather peaceful to-day, as the Seventh-Day Adventists have gone to church. Luckily there is not much more that we can do at present.

" Is it not strange that on this small island, and on this sandy, deserted beach which stretches for miles, covered a few yards inland with thick scrub, we should find, not twenty yards away, a tombstone in excellent preservation, with the following inscription ?

TO THE MEMORY
OF
ALEXANDER MACLARTY, M.D.
FELLOW OF THE ROYAL COLLEGE OF
PHYSICIANS, EDINBURGH,
AND LATE DIRECTOR OF THE VACCINE
ESTABLISHMENT OF THE ISLAND OF JAMAICA
AND PHYSICIAN TO THE PUBLIC HOSPITAL OF
THE CITY OF KINGSTON IN THAT ISLAND ;

WHO DEPARTED THIS LIFE
ON BOARD THE WALSINGHAM PACKET
ON THE 4TH APRIL 1821
ON HIS PASSAGE TO GREAT BRITAIN,
IN THE 46TH YEAR OF HIS AGE.

HE WAS
A GENTLEMAN OF SCRUPULOUS HONOUR
AND INTEGRITY ; ZEALOUS AND FEELING
IN THE DISCHARGE OF HIS PROFESSIONAL DUTIES ;
AND MOST EXEMPLARY IN ALL HIS
OTHER RELATIONS IN LIFE.

A FOND AND AFFECTIONATE
HUSBAND, FATHER AND BROTHER
AND
A WARM-HEARTED, STEADY AND
SINCERE FRIEND.

———

THIS INADEQUATE TRIBUTE IS INSCRIBED
IN AFFECTIONATE REMEMBRANCE
BY
HIS WIDOW.

" ' Inadequate Tribute ! '

" The local mail-steamer which runs between Nassau and these islands arrived this afternoon. She is named *Alisada* and, in addition to her sails, has Diesel engines. We are therefore more optimistic. The Captain, a coloured man, struck me as being most efficient, and, judging by his size, should have no trouble in getting his orders carried out. He had received a message from Nassau through a lighthouse to render us what assistance he could. He loaned us a heavy anchor and chain-cable, which we laid out, and he joined a rope to our cable and prepared to try towing us off.

" I went with him aboard his ship and, as it was after dark, kept up communication with those on board *Tai-Mo-Shan* by flashlight. He failed to move her, and we realised that we will not do so until we get ' rollers ' and ' skids ' under her. Owing to the angle at which she is lying, this is no easy matter, even if they could be procured here. We are going to make every effort to improve matters by Tuesday, when he returns from Inagua, which *Alisada* has to visit in the meanwhile. The villagers were procured again to haul on the purchase in unison with the towing effort of the schooner.

They have gone now, leaving just the five of us on this beach which we are getting to know so well. Red is busy also writing a diary on the opposite side of the wood fire. The tide is just about high now and is lapping around *Tai-Mo-Shan's* bow ; it does seem so absurd that we cannot float her. Our urgent need at the moment is for jacks, skids and rollers. To bed, ready for to-morrow's work ; I find the sun, fresh air and work combine to make one ready for sleep at an absurdly early hour.

" *Sunday*, 18*th February*.

" We have had the most strenuous day of the lot to-day. Helped by the Seventh-Day Adventists, we proceeded to build a breakwater to serve the double purpose of protecting the vessel and enabling us to dig under her keel to place rollers and skids. We have made this breakwater by lashing together piles in an intricate network, resulting in a breakwater some ten-foot across. The centre is filled with sand, while the sides are plugged up with seaweed to prevent fresh sand and water from destroying the work. The breakwater is completed from the starboard bow to half-way down that side, while on the port side it extends even further. I took charge of the pole supply ; each one represents a palmetto which has had to be chopped down with a hatchet, the palm-leaves at the top lopped off and then dragged by hand across the sand to the boat. Gradually we exhausted the supplies of good wood in the vicinity and had to transport them through the thick undergrowth for about a mile. However, it is well worth the labour, as Red, George and Philip have produced a massive-looking structure.

"We are all absolutely dog-tired this evening. Bertie has had to spend a day on his bed, such as it is, owing to a large boil on his thigh. To-night at supper one of the natives produced some bark which, when boiled, produced a tea of light-pink hue. They call it 'brazaleeta' (spelt as they pronounce it here). Quite good, but does not touch Indian or China tea for flavour! A small sailing-schooner, the *Louise*, which anchored in here from the weather to-day, has renewed our hopes of soon having the vessel afloat. Her Captain has promised to leave as soon as the weather moderates for Acklin, an island some fifty miles away, to fetch their father with jacks, rollers, skids, etc., and swearing that to refloat the boat will be an easy matter. The question of money is to be fixed on his arrival here. We are very hopeful.

"*Monday, 19th February*.

"A windy night. All had a very disturbed sleep, but signs of rain last night came to nothing. Was awakened at daylight by 'Uncle John.' Found the breakwater on the starboard side completely washed away by the high tide last night. We must not be defeated, so John and I set off to a point about a mile away, which we have not yet cleared of palmettos. We worked like slaves until 10.30, by which time we had as many as the others could cope with. I found the remains of a house near the point, which John told me dated from the slavery days. The walls are so stoutly built of brick that it has stood there despite tidal waves and hurricanes, many of which must have expended their wrath in vain upon it!

"We must be getting a proper shipwrecked appearance by now, shaving and washing being things of the past, while our clothes, owing to repeated soakings, are falling to pieces. One could dispense with them altogether were it not for the presence of so many of the village females, and at night-time the cold makes them a necessity.

" There is a grass here known as bird-grass, with the most painful prickles, which hinders the tree-felling a great deal. I have taken to shoes again for this reason. By the end of to-day we have a strong breakwater built up on the port side of the ship, which should stand up to the sea ; it certainly seems to be having the effect of causing the sand to be washed away from the port side, which is a good thing.

" *Tuesday, 20th February.*

" Breakwater has held well throughout the night. ' Uncle Ben ' and I laid out anchors afresh and weighted them down with every conceivable thing, and also placed them in rock crevices, leaving nothing to chance. Wind went round to south-west, which is what we do not want as this is from seaward and brings in a nasty swell and breaking sea which is liable to endanger the rudder. However, Philip and George to-day combatted this by lashing battens, etc., to the rudder, and appear to have made a good job of it. This forenoon we hauled everything taut and ready for the arrival of *Alisada.* She seemed to be in a hurry to get going away, and after lengthy discussion Red went off in her to Nassau, to arrange for assistance ; he should arrive there on Friday.

" *Wednesday: 21st February.*

" Last night was terrible, sleep being practically impossible, owing to the activities of sand-flies. The wind had dropped, leaving them in charge, and they did their job so thoroughly that we sat in the smoke of a fire, scratching, scratching, scratching ! However, at about 3 a.m. McKinney arrived to tell us that he was prepared to start for Long Cay, some thirteen miles away, which I was eager to reach, owing to the reported presence of jacks, skids, etc. The Commissioner, a coloured man, had spent some time with us last night, and had confirmed this rumour, so I had told McKinney that I would go there at any time.

" We got going in his small sailing-boat by 4 a.m. ; his son completed the party of three, and the wind falling light it was not until seven-thirty that we arrived off Long Cay. I was desperately tired, but cramped conditions did not allow of anything but sudden dropping off to sleep and equally sudden awakenings. Long Cay was larger than Landrail Point, and had at one time experienced a certain prosperity, even boasting a wireless station. The latter is to be closed shortly, as its upkeep is no longer justified in a place where the remains of fallen houses and piles of rocks and masonry, still serve as a terrible reminder of the hurricanes and tidal waves which have devastated it. I had a note to the local constable and carpenter. These jobs were combined and were carried out by a coloured man of large size and cheerful disposition. At about eleven-thirty we got going again on the return journey ; in addition to McKinney, his son and myself, we also had two locals who wished to view *Tai-Mo-Shan*, also a load of cocoanut-palm rollers, two jacks, prises, etc., and—lots of added optimism.

The journey back took from 11.30 a.m. to 6.30 p.m.

under a baking sun. We were not allowed to get dejected, for one of our passengers was the native who had been in charge of the wireless station. Mr. Toote was a man for whom at sheer persuasive argument it would be hard to find an equal. He practised his talents on McKinney, a recent convert to the Seventh-Day way of thinking, and, as he could quote from the Bible with ease, he often had his rival outclassed. I forget now all that was proved, but it was most entertaining and kept me from dropping asleep among the rollers at the bottom of the boat on several occasions. Many very controversial points were finally settled after lengthy quotations to Mr. Toote's satisfaction. However, as a verbal duel it would have done credit to many of our eminent lawyers. Missionaries have certainly not been idle among the natives of these islands.

" Meanwhile the other three were busy at *Tai-Mo-Shan* settlement getting the warps, anchors and other tackle ready for renewed efforts on my return with the gear. If only we can get her off before Red has to get assistance from Nassau it will be grand, as that is bound to mean great expense, whereas the loan of this gear to-day has only cost me ten shillings. We *must* succeed.

" The Commissioner, a well-educated coloured man, told me a good story last night. A predecessor of his who was on tour, visiting the settlements on other islands, sent a note back to his headquarters to the headman of that settlement, in order to get a book that he required from his office. He explained in the note that it might be on his desk, a large office one, but that should it not be there, he must look in the bookshelf on the wall.   So careful were his instructions and so conscientious was the recipient of this letter, that the Commissioner was rewarded, a few days later, by the arrival of a boat which contained the book, the desk and the bookshelf.

"Very tired, so am sleeping at McKinney's house in the settlement to-night, to escape the sand-flies."

CHAPTER XVII

Our Salvage Efforts Successful

The journal continues :

> " *Tuesday, 22nd February.*

" I slept at McK.'s house, a one-floored wooden shack which was very warm, and owing to the absence of Mrs. McK. at Nassau, I had a double-bed to myself and an excellent rest. I arrived down here at sunrise this morning, to find that Bertie and George, to escape the sand-flies, had shared our canvas boat for a bed, while Philip had commandeered one of the local skiffs. They all pushed off some way from the shore. I think both B. and G. must have found their quarters somewhat confined, but they assured me that they were soon asleep where sand-flies could not bother them. Their night's rest was rudely disturbed by the boat, which proved to have a small leak, filling with water, and they had now decided that, as a bed, the boat was one hundred per cent. inefficient. They had spent the rest of the night rather miserably on the beach.

" To-day we started with high hopes of success and, owing to the return of the schooner *Louise* from Acklin Island, we now had three jacks and a sufficient number of rollers and planks.

" Of our terrific efforts I shall not write in too much detail, except to note that, now the evening has arrived, we are all ready for bed and are talking over ways and means to defeat these confounded sand-flies. We started off this morning by placing all three jacks under her stern, in order to lift her sufficiently to get a roller under her keel. This took a long time, as it entailed setting them in position within a very confined area between the rudder and the ships's bottom, with water frequently washing over our heads. We did get a roller under the keel and skids under this roller. The rollers under the bilge were an easier matter, as were the skids, which went under them. These ' skids ' were two-inch planks which were placed fore-and-aft under the rollers, thus preventing the latter from sinking down into the sand.

" We then set two of the ' jacks ' up against the stern and, having by this time obtained the help of the villagers, proceeded to screw up on them while hauling on the purchase, which was attached to the hawsers. These ran out to the cable to which the anchors were attached. The hawser attached to the cable got bar taut. We waited anxiously for the jacks to reveal a sign of motion. The long line of natives who stretched away up the beach past our encampment kept a steady strain on the hawser. Suddenly laughter rang out ; these natives had fallen to the ground as the hawser came home with a run. Examination with a water-glass soon detected the broken link in the cable loaned us by the mail-boat. We rejoined the cable with a shackle and off we started again. If only she would lift upon the rollers, she had to go !

" We waited impatiently for the next haul, during the overhauling of the purchase. The villagers, feeling the effects of the hot sun, were beginning to take less interest in the proceedings. Their efforts suffered in consequence. The wind determined to defeat our optimism and began to freshen from seaward. Another pull, another sickening wrench, and again a slackening of everything. This time a seven-inch hawser had parted. This capped our efforts, and we decided to talk over our next step. Meanwhile, on the ' blind ' or seaward side of the boat, a dozen men were given the job of prizing under the keel. This entailed getting the point of a long pole under the keel and then, by sitting along its length, assisting the jacks to lift. They were sitting in a row, obviously blessing their luck at having got such an easy number, when, with a loud snap, the pole broke in two and all of them were flung ignominiously into the sea. ' Out of sight—out of mind ' was never more applicable, for until the dripping figures began to appear one by one around the stern, we had forgotten their presence. They all laughed ; everybody does, here !

" Before going to bed to-night we have decided to give the Captain of *Louise* a free hand, and are offering him a sum to get her off in twenty-four hours. He seems most capable and confident of success. He has been spinning stories to us to-night about his own shipwrecks. Owing to the very sudden changes of wind both in force and direction, it is no unusual occurrence in this part of the world for sailing-vessels to run ashore, and so these schooner captains are excellent at salvage. He amused us with a story of how he got wrecked around the shores of Cuba on one occasion in a small boat. His expenses after refloating her were overwhelming. They charged him seventy-five dollars for vaccinating him and his crew, which was a compulsory matter, of course. Similar sums were constantly required of him, until at last he found that it would be cheaper to quit the vessel than pay them. He left with his crew at one in the morning, and so I suppose that the officials, who were due next morning to collect the money, found only a deserted boat. He seems a good fellow and well able to take charge of the native labour. To somebody's plaintive cry of 'Mind my fingers, boss,' he replied, 'Why, you've plenty more !' We also notice that he has a knack of employing the younger men on the more exacting jobs, while those of a lighter nature fall to the lot of ' Uncle Ben ' and ' Prince ' and their contemporaries, who must be well on in the seventies.

"McKinney regaled some of the younger natives with a story yesterday. He was serving in a sailing-schooner in his youth, and they traded around the coasts of South America. When this incident took place they were off the coast of Colombia. He commenced his story by saying, ' And do you know, boys, I was once at a place where we bought turtles from the natives without saying nothing on either side ? ' A moment's silence followed to allow the importance of this statement to sink into their woolly heads. ' It happened in this fashion,' he continued. ' There was a reef some distance off shore and, though there was an opening through it, so rough was the water that ships were not in the habit of entering by this channel. Well, we would put our money into bottles and throw them into the sea. The natives ashore waited for them to be washed up on the beach. They would then see how many

turtles were required by the amount of money inside.
They got the turtles in pairs, and to each pair they
fastened a cork buoy. Now turtles, I don't know
whether you know it or not, but anyhow it is a fact,
always pull contrary like to each other. They would
release a pair, and they always tried to get to the open
sea, which meant that they had to pass through the
opening which I have already told you existed. As they
swam along they would constantly be disappearing
from view and taking the buoy with them. They soon
got tired, owing to this habit of pulling contrary-like
to the other, and the buoy would reappear. It was then
easy for us to get in the boats and secure our money's-
worth. Of course this was in a way illegal, because
these turtles were all owned, and the natives were just
making a little money on their own. Our captain was
eager to make a good profit by getting plenty of them.
We were found by another ship who asked us what we
were doing with these turtles, and though she herself
had no more right to them than we had, she took from
us all we had collected in the boats. We were a faster
ship, and so we sailed away with plenty of turtles that
we had already put on board.'

"The local names here are picturesque. Hark at
these—Crooked Island, Landrail Point, Albert Town,
Long Cay, Spring Point, Pompey Bay, Delectable Bay,
Selina Point, Mason Bay, China Hill, Snug Corner, and
Marine Farm (of which I have already written).

"After work to-day we are still optimistic, so we
have sent a signal by Toote to Long Cay, where there is
a wireless station, to Red at Nassau, asking him to wait
until further orders before making any definite salvage

contract. He should get it on his arrival there to-morrow.

"*Friday*, 23*rd February*.

"Captain Collie of the *Louise* got busy early. I had again slept under the McKinneys' roof, while the others preferred the deck of the *Louise*, about a quarter of a mile from the shore. To-day the crew of the *Louise*, helped by the locals, worked on the for'ard end of the boat. The plan was to haul her bow round into the sea, instead of trying to haul her off stern first, as we have been attempting to do until now. By about noon he had the bow well jacked up and several rollers and skids under the foremost end of the keel and under the bow. He also placed two jacks under her port bow to help push it to seaward. She was listed heavily over to port, but the weather luckily has remained fine and the sea calm.

"Despite repeated haulings we did not get the initial start on her, though the jacks have moved her bow slightly to seaward. Two anchors were laid out in the starboard bow, the inner end of the cable being joined to the purchase by the remains of the seven-inch hawser. This again parted.

"It is now 9 p.m. and all is quiet except for the chirping of numerous crickets in the bush behind this camp. A bright moon lights up one boat which is lying on her port side, some twenty yards from where I am stretched out on the sand, with an oil lamp to enable me to write up this diary. Bertie is in his sleeping-bag alongside me, while from a short distance away come the sounds of the voices of the other two, doubtless discussing the day's events. It is high tide at 1 a.m. and all the men are to be here to haul by then.

" *Saturday, 24th February.*

" I am extremely glad, as, indeed, we all are, to note that, as I write now at 1 p.m., the bow no longer points up the beach but inclines slightly out to sea. The raucous shout of Ben Gibson, a huge native, ' O.K. Haul away ' is drifting into my tent, a true indication of the spirit of confidence which has taken possession of everyone.

" The excited chatter of the women makes concentration difficult, while the men all have that I-told-you-so air, even though they have been here since one o'clock this morning. She is still turning to starboard, but I think that soon Captain Collie will shift the anchor cables, now coming in on the starboard quarter of the vessel, on to the starboard bow.

" We started off by meeting down here at 1 a.m., but on this occasion we employed the men only, feeling that it was scarcely a fair hour at which to expect the womenfolk to turn out. We found that high tide was at about 3.30 a.m. this morning, and by 2.30 we were getting ready for it. The men pulled with a good will, but despite the luff which we used in order to get the maximum results from their efforts, we were getting pretty desperate about our chances by 5 a.m. And then—Can we move that bow ?—No, sir !—we decide to keep on for a few more minutes. The marvellous happens. She starts. No, it can't be true !—must be the coming dawn which is deceiving us—we lean a stick against the port bow, with a few inches protruding above the gunwale. Can it be true that those inches are decreasing ?—let's move nearer up the rope and get a clearer view in this cursed half-light—I wish that man would pull on this rope instead of cursing us all—my fingers ache and feel as though I can never straighten them out again. I wish I had not cursed Arthur, the cook, for being late in arriving this morning. He is next to me on the rope. He eyes me furtively, rather sulkily, but he too is pulling, pulling. I hear Philip's voice somewhere at the back—' One, two, six, HAUL AWAY !' I didn't know he could raise such a roar ; I see George's scarlet sweater over Arthur's shoulder moving forward, backward, forward, backward. A shout, a cheer, as the stick falls. ' She moves !' is shouted by everyone, rather to give relief to their feelings than to inform their neighbour of such an obvious fact. ' Hold it and rest,' shouts Captain Collie. . . .

" I had no sleep last night, owing to these sandflies, and I was glad when we decided to cease work for the forenoon and continue at 1 p.m. This sun has blistered my lips, which are giving me agony, while all of us have sore feet, sore hands, and many abrasions. Bertie has been suffering from boils. It will be grand to get settled aboard again. The amount of gear that is damaged is going to be expensive to replace. Last night we again broke the hawser attached to the cable on the port bow, so promptly replaced it with a shackle of cable from the anchors on the starboard quarter. This resulted in the breaking of a fluke on our own anchor, which had in turn to be replaced by a heavier anchor of Captain Collie's. Of course it all takes time in small open boats, but the water is so clear that we can do a good deal of the shackling and unshackling under water. We are hoping for even better results by this evening.

"7 p.m.

"We have not advanced much, owing to shackles, anchors and cable parting. We have a collection of fractured specimens now. We are trying again at 2 a.m. to-morrow.

"*Sunday, 25th February,* 9 a.m.

"I slept at McKinney's house again until 1.30 a.m., when I was awakened by the alarm-clock which I had taken there for the purpose. I have only heard of one clock in the whole village, and that one is owned by a sick old man who would scarcely wish to be awakened at these early hours. We gradually mustered down here, and as a result *Tai-Mo-Shan* is facing out to sea. We are now struggling to slide her into the deeper water by which her bow is already surrounded.

"We are trying to keep the men at it until we have completed it, but I am afraid that, both by the emptiness of their stomachs and the height of the sun, they realise that it is their breakfast time. Owing to the absence of clocks, to which I have referred, all time is reckoned by the height of the sun, which seems to suit their requirements. All directions are referred to by the points of the compass, and instead of 'Move over to the right or left,' you will hear, 'Move over to the north or south.'

"Last night a cable arrived at Long Cay and has come from there by boat, telling us that Red has a tug ready at Nassau. I am confident that this will not be necessary now, and when she reaches deep water we can signal him that all is well.

"*Later.*

"Delaying operations until this evening's high tide at about 4 p.m.

" 6 p.m.

" We have wasted rather a lot of time at this high tide, with the result that we have ended up with the anchors embedded firmly in rock. Up to now every time the villagers hauled, the anchors came home. We must now postpone events until 4 a.m. to-morrow. Surely we *must* go this time. Being pretty well fagged out every evening, we are glad to get to bed. Starting in the early hours of the morning and working throughout the day in a hot sun makes one ready for bed. Unfortunately we are plagued by flies during the day and by sand-flies at night. Bertie is confined to bed with boils these days, and the rest of us are suffering from numerous abrasions.

" There is the quaintest little fellow in the *Louise*. From his size he would appear to be about three years old, but he has an elderly, little face, black as your hat, and a very solemn way of talking. George and I were in conversation with him this evening during a lull in the hauling proceedings. The girls of the village chatted away merrily to each other over the rope. In answer to our queries as to what he thought of the young ladies of this settlement, he said, ' They seem to make laughter of me, but I am no gamester.' When we asked him if he was ever seasick aboard the small schooner, he said, ' I have never been seasick since I was born, but I quite often pray to be sick.' On noticing our surprise at his wish to be seasick, he added, ' My chest gets so dirty, I long to be sick.' On asking him his age, he replied with great solemnity, ' I really do not know ; my mother has never told me.'

" *Monday, 26th February.*   9 p.m.

" I slept at McKinney's again last night, and though
I offered the others the use of the bed, they admitted
that they preferred to risk the sand-flies to a trudge of
about a mile and a half through the sand. I have rather
enjoyed the experience of sleeping up there the last few
nights. I usually walk up with Ben Gibson. He is a
great hulking native, rather morose, who needs careful
handling. However, when acting as host, he is very
polite, though he always manages to put in a request for
a gift of food or rope. They find the latter very hard to
obtain and are in great need of it for their boats.

" We have had wonderful moonlit nights, and
trudging through the sand with weary feet, I have been
refreshed by the absolute beauty of the evenings. The
starlit sky and silvery sea, the long stretch of yellow
sand and the palm-trees silhouetted against the sky make
a scene which the most matter-of-fact person could not
fail to note. The houses in the settlement, which have
white walls and are approached by paths bestrewn with
large boulders, thrown up there by the last tidal wave,
show up clear-cut in the moonlight. Scarcely a sound
is to be heard. Occasionally muffled voices and merry
laughter proclaim the fact that even though the parents
may go to bed early, the spirit of youth cannot be
damped so easily ! Each evening I would stop at Ben's
house and smoke a cigarette, while one of his daughters
was sent to get two glasses of water. This water is a
great delicacy, as the tidal wave has sent the wells
brackish, but Ben has installed a tank and is able to drink
pure rain-water. By the time I usually reach my host's
dwelling, he is in bed, and a sleepy voice calls out :

' Please come round to the East door ! ' My host is a great Seventh-Day Adventist, and his religious beliefs adhere strictly to the letter of the Bible. I notice that even the damage done to the West door by a hurricane has been repaired by a coloured sheet which illustrates the doings of Jeroboam. All the reading-matter is of a religious nature, but so fatigued am I on arrival there that I have no time for improving my knowledge thereby.

" This morning, being in possession of the alarm-clock, I again became the village caller, and, having awakened my host and his two sons, I proceeded to John's house, by way of Ben's, the latter acknowledging my ' rouser ' with a grunt. They were expecting me, as a large mug of tea, with sugar, and biscuits stood ready on the table. I found them all in the kitchen, a separate one-roomed building which adjoined their living quarters.

" A wood-fire luckily filled the place with smoke and served to hide my astonishment when ' Poppa ' remarked in front of his wife, and five of the six children, that he was kind of feeling that we were going to get off this time, and that he would not meet the five of us again until we were in Heaven ! I felt that such God-fearing people are somewhat better-equipped to enter those realms than one so ill-prepared as myself. However, I am glad to say that the first half of his prediction came true !

" We have had another tiring day. The boat did come off into deep waters fairly easily, but having got clear of the beach and still having on a heavy list, we proceeded to examine the ship's side. We found one plank on the port side crushed in. Some of the coppering is worn away, but is in one small area amidships. We were glad to be able to signal Red that the damage was slight and that we were afloat once more, and will be sailing for Nassau to-morrow. While we were putting a patch on the damaged plank, the wind freshened considerably and threatened to blow from seaward. We had to work our way out through the passage in the reef, which necessitated both skilful placing and frequent shifting of the anchors, by which we hauled ourselves out. While doing this we had to keep the list on the boat, to get her through the shallow water, and did so by attaching anchors to the end of the starboard spinnaker boom. At one period, owing to a delay in tripping the anchors, we became rather anxious, and were all most relieved when at about 4 p.m. we finally anchored well clear to seaward of the reef.

"By dark *Tai-Mo-Shan* settlement had ceased to exist, though most of it still remained on the upper deck. Supper was a very cheerful meal, as we were all in the best of spirits, and Captain Collie, accompanied by three of his crew, came to supper. The natives of these islands were brought over as slaves from West Africa, and to-night Captain Collie himself told us the following story. He said that his great-grandfather lived in West Africa, and that the British found out that he was very fond of peanuts. They laid a trail of them, and grandpa found them much to his liking. One day he came to the end of the trail, and there he found some British officials, holding out a bag of peanuts. Captain Collie explained that his great-grandfather, not knowing how to use his hands, popped his head into the bag to obtain what he wanted. No sooner had he done so than a string was pulled tightly around his neck. They took him by ship to Acklin Island in the Bahamas, where they released him and told him that he was to start a new life, and that in future his name was Adam Collie. That is how, the Captain explained, his family got their name and came to live on Acklin Island."

CHAPTER XVIII

We Leave Crooked Island for Nassau

The following day, Tuesday, 27th February, we spent in stowing provisions, stores and clothing. Everything was full of sand, but we wasted no time in getting our belongings down below, as we were anxious to be out of these waters. Luckily it kept fine, but no sooner had we got the upper-deck cleared than several heavy rain-squalls followed each other in quick succession. We paid off the natives, and besides the money that was due to them we gave them considerable amounts of rope and provisions. John Gibson and his son Bryan were the last to leave us, and as we weighed anchor tears streamed down their black faces. Poppa remarked that we had never been treated so well before ! In fact, at Nassau we received the following letter :

> " Landrail Point,
> Bird Rock.

From Master Bryan L. Gibson,
    1934, March 6.

" Well, Dear Sir I sat down with much pleurique (pleasure ?) to write you all know that I am still well and I wanted to know how you all manged (managed) go in down in Nassau if you all had a good time or a bad time I was very sorrow when we was to part also tell the captain mate cook and purcer amd doctor farther say must tell them thousand houdy.[1] But I was very glad when you all got her of cookry pleas let me know how you mange and I also hope to hear from you all when you get home to England. I all so hope to hear from you on this mail tell the Bosin I look to hear from them too Also rember me to the Captain Mr. Mate, Boisin Doctor I hope you all me send me so candy for me. don't forget the pictures. So plenty you time know plenty to talk But time is short

From you ever Dear friend
Bryan L. Gibson."

Just before sunset we sailed past the lighthouse and dipped our ensign in final salutation to the island where these adventures had befallen us. We sailed up the channel with Long Island to port, Rum Cay and Conception Island to starboard. At daylight next morning we sighted Devil Point, the south-west corner of Cat Island. We were very short of charts and other navigational aids, as we had forwarded them to Nassau to prevent damage. At noon we were abreast the island of Little San Salvador, where we hove-to, in a freshening wind and a series of rain-squalls, to check our position. Having done so, we made for the open sea, passing, to do so, between Little San Salvador Island to the southward and the southern end of Eleuthera Island to the northward.

No sooner were we clear of these islands than we experienced unpleasant weather conditions. The following night was a miserable one in consequence. The inside of the boat presented a depressing appearance,

---

[1] Native word for " best wishes ".

with wet clothes underfoot and a large quantity of sand everywhere which had insisted on accompanying us from Crooked Island. We had on board the heavy cable which we had borrowed from the mail-boat, and this we were now taking down to Nassau. We had stowed it on the deck of the saloon, as the proper stowage under the deck was occupied by our own cable. The added weight caused the boat to ride much heavier than usual, and we took over some pretty solid seas.

At daylight on Tuesday we were surprised to find no sign of Eleuthera Island ; the wind from the north-east had abated slightly, and was then blowing about force 6-7, while a heavy sea was running. We decided to remain on a northerly course until 8 a.m. before closing the land. We then proceeded to alter course, and we were greatly relieved when land was spied from aloft in the first dog-watch. By means of the pilot hand-book we were able to identify our landfall as Great Egg Island. By 5.15 that evening we were abreast of this island, which left us some thirty-odd miles to Nassau light ; and our alteration for this harbour, of course, put the sea astern.

Our entrance here was not without its excitement. We had only one chart of this harbour, and on it one could cover the whole of New Providence Island, on which Nassau is situated, with a thumbnail. However, we drew up our plans of attack, and by 11 p.m., having taken the precaution of lowering the mainsail, we were rapidly approaching the light at the entrance. We crossed the bar without mishap, though we could not observe one of the buoys which marked the entrance. It was not until afterwards that we heard that it had recently been rammed and sunk. As soon as the buoyed channel became too narrow to allow of us beating up it, we dropped the kedge anchor, our own heavier anchor having been damaged at Crooked Island. We rapidly proceeded to drag. Luckily the heavy mailboat's anchor had been got ready, but by the time we got it overboard we were in close proximity to a bunch of rocks. For several anxious moments we prayed that it would hold. The leadsman kept singing out in true naval style, " Ship going astern, Sir,' and we were greatly relieved, after what seemed an age, to hear him shout, " Ship stopped, Sir."

We decided that the position was too unhealthy a one to allow of sound sleep, and we pulled ashore in our boat to arrange a tow. This was not necessary, as a launch soon drew up alongside. They had mistaken us for one of the yachts which were competing in the Miami to Nassau race. Only three out of fourteen yachts arrived at Nassau, the remainder having turned back on account of the weather. The Committee launch very kindly towed us up harbour, despite the mistake that they had made, and we were secured alongside the pier at Symonette's shipbuilding yard. Ryder now rejoined us, and we enjoyed a most welcome night's rest. The distance from Crooked Island was 279 miles, which we had covered at a daily average of 121 miles. Unfortunately, on anchoring that evening, Francis had received a sharp blow from the cable, which was to cause him a great deal of trouble and to prolong our stay both here and at Bermuda.

We arranged for *Tai-Mo-Shan* to be taken in hand for repairs. The damage was by no means extensive, and only entailed the replacing of two planks and the renewing of some of the Muntz-metal plates which covered the bottom. We also took this opportunity of repainting and revarnishing the vessel. We painted out the interior ourselves, so that by the time she left the slipway all sand and other traces of our grounding had been removed. We were nearly in trouble once more however. We were at anchor one day in Nassau Harbour, when a strong wind caused her to strain at her cable. It finally blew with such force that we decided to shift billet further inshore, where better protection from the storm was afforded us. Hardly had we weighed anchor than we proceeded to go shooting down the harbour under the combined force of wind and tide. What followed must have appeared a most awkward display of seamanship to the spectators aboard numerous other and more luxurious yachts, until the truth was known. As soon as we had found that we were unable to combat the force of the elements in the limited space at our disposal, we dropped our anchor again. We were then well clear of other vessels at anchor, but we were horrified to find that our anchor failed to hold us. We were swept down by the tide at an ever-increasing speed. The cable rattled and shook, but still the anchor failed to hold. We felt helpless, and rather self-conscious as the guests aboard a particularly large steam-yacht, close to which we were sweeping at the moment, hurried across the deck to watch the fun.

We were heading for the *Vamarie*, the winner of the Miami race. She had a beautifully-varnished side which glistened in the sunshine. We held our breath.

By some stroke of good fortune we just managed to avoid her, and passed close to the slipway on Hog Island, where we had just completed repairs. We weighed the cable and found that our anchor flukes had parted. Evidently the hard usage to which they had been put during our grounding had strained them. Fortunately a Diesel-engined oil lighter, seeing our plight, hurried out to our assistance. We then secured to a buoy, which ended our troubles.

I think that this and similar incidents during our voyage made one realise that an engine would be of great use. I do not mean that one should convert one's vessel into a motor-cruiser. The two forms of sport are entirely different, but in these days when small and reliable marine engines can be purchased at such a moderate price, I think that an engine of a few horse-power will pay for itself many times over by virtue of the money which it saves in repairs. An engine of this nature would undoubtedly have saved us from grounding at Crooked Island, and as our repairs and payment of labour together totalled about eighty pounds, I think it would have justified its existence. The reason that we did not fit an engine in the first place was the extra weight and space which it would occupy. I do not think that all yachtsmen could expect to be so lucky as we were, for on nearing harbour entrances a tug of some sort was nearly always put at our disposal. The American Navy were responsible for this courtesy at all the American ports that we visited. As I have mentioned elsewhere, we were also extremely fortunate in being provided with a tow free-of-charge through the Panama Canal.

Also anchored in the harbour at Nassau was the little yacht *May*, on board which was Group-Captain Rees, who wears among many others the most coveted of all decorations, the Victoria Cross. I spent an evening on board with him, and it is one which I shall long remember. We talked till the early hours of the morning, and he discoursed at length on the numerous evidences of the wanderings of the Israelites, which he had discovered by observation from air-planes when commanding the Air Force in Transjordania. His little boat was most comfortable, and it interested me to hear of his voyage from England. He had left from Falmouth and sailed to Nassau, stopping at the Azores *en route*. This journey, undertaken absolutely unaccompanied, had taken him ninety-five days. When the time came for me to return to my own vessel, so rough was it that a trip in the canvas boat would possibly have had a fatal ending. I slept on board his ship, and I was amused when, next morning, he insisted on getting under way to take me across the harbour. His routine for leaving harbour was an orderly one. He started up his engine and, leaving it in neutral, went forward to the small double-barrelled winch on which he weighed his two anchors, the handles and other gear for the purpose being of a simple nature. He then hurried to the cockpit, from which he could control his engine and also adjust the setting of his sails as necessary. The simplicity of the whole manoeuvre further impressed on me the advantage of having an engine for entering or leaving harbours or small anchorages.

The cost of living at Nassau was extremely high, and indeed would have proved ruinous had not the fluctuations of the American dollar been in our favour at the time. On arrival, the baths which we so badly required after our exertions at Crooked Island cost us the equivalent of eight shillings a head. Hair-cuts were on the same scale, and as the five of us were on half-pay we decided to look for cheaper quarters. One of the crew did live on board, but as two planks on the ship's side had had to be removed on the port side, and the interior was receiving a fresh coat of paint throughout, living conditions there were of a low order. However, we were lucky to find amidst all the display of wealth a comfortable little hotel which catered for our wants at most reasonable prices. No less eminent a person than Al Capone had previously patronised the place when enjoying the fruits of his labours. We were amused to hear stories of his sea-bathing while at Nassau, as, when he crossed the sands, a stalwart bodyguard formed a ring around their master, and also accompanied him into the sea.

Owing to the efficient manner in which Pan-American Airways are conducted, Nassau is of easy access to Americans from around Miami and other places on the coasts of Florida. A continuous service of fast and luxurious tourist-liners also adds to its prosperity. The attractions of the seas around the Bahama Islands are numerous. The coral reefs, the clearness of the water, the many-coloured tropical fish, all combined to make our stay there a most enjoyable one, while the places of historical interest were not the least of its many charms. So much hospitality was extended to us here that we decided that we must endeavour to show our appreciation of it. This took the form of a cocktail-party. For this purpose we moored the boat alongside a jetty which normally served as a landing-place for passengers arriving there by launch to view the gardens. We used a summer-house as a refreshment-bar. I think that our guests found it a rather original party in that we served the sixty or seventy of them ourselves, which was rather different to the large staff employed for this purpose at the other functions of a similar nature which we had attended. In fact, a very high official was heard to remark that he had never before drunk whisky-and-soda out of a beer-mug in public !

There are many adventurous spirits to be met with at these seaports. Such a one was a young Englishman who called on board one evening. He had been a clerk in the Foreign Office in London, and his dreams of adventure had caused him to throw up his job, persuade a friend to do the same, and together they bought a small sailing-boat. This did not leave them with much money by the time that they had sailed her across the Atlantic to the Bahamas. In fact, they had only sufficient for their immediate needs. The two of them then decided that more money must be raised before the journey could be carried further. They tossed a coin to decide who should remain with the boat and who should seek some remunerative employment in America. Our friend, having lost, had journeyed to the States, where he found little difficulty in earning money by navigating duties aboard yachts. Meanwhile his friend was adding a little to their meagre resources by selling cocoanuts. When we were at Nassau he was navigator of a large sailing-ship which was engaged in taking moving-pictures of under-water life around these islands, while a sunken galleon would, it was hoped, yield up some treasure. While we were actually here a whale entered through the reef and was shot. It was secured alongside this ship and was later towed out to sea, to be used in their pictures.

When we reached Nassau we were all in rather a pitiable condition. It was not until the vessel had been safely refloated that the strain began to tell on her crew. Sand-fly bites and abrasions, aggravated by the heat and almost continuous immersion in salt water, had made the wearing of shoes a matter of great discomfort, while other portions of our anatomy suffered as well. By the time that treatment at hospital had sufficiently cured Francis, who had unfortunately been obliged to spend his time there, the rest of us were in sound condition once more. We sailed for Bermuda on the twenty-third of March, after an enjoyable stay of three weeks.

Head winds still continued on our passage from Nassau to Bermuda, and we had some difficulty in consequence in making Bermuda. We arrived there on the first of April, our average for this thousand miles being just over one hundred miles a day. Our arrival there concluded a stretch of the voyage from Colon which had involved sailing close-hauled for nearly 3,000 miles, during which it was only possible to sail off the wind for a period of two days. This leg of the voyage was uneventful, but we were gratified to find that our vessel was making excellent headway to windward, a great improvement being noticeable in her speed now that our stores were considerably reduced. When we were nine miles from Bermuda a signal was passed to us by semaphore from the Commander-in-Chief of the West

Indies Station, Admiral the Hon. Sir Reginald Plunkett-Drax, K.C.B. Such a warm welcome was expressed in this signal that we were eager to arrive there. When we approached the naval dockyard, we saw that the flagship H.M.S. *Norfolk* was moored alongside the dockyard wall. We were berthed close astern of her, and we received a great ovation from her ship's company and officers. In fact, our stay here was marked by a series of festivities which continued until we finally set sail again.

Owing to the delay which had been occasioned by the grounding, coupled with the fact that Francis's leg had had to receive attention in hospital, we intended to make our stay here of only three days' duration. This was not to be, however. Further trouble with this leg arose, and again necessitated hospital treatment. We all felt sorry for him, but inwardly we were rather pleased, I think, at the excuse for staying at Bermuda that his illness gave us. It was a month before the sick man was fit enough to accompany us, but we were determined to wait for him. Many of our friends had doubted our ability to perform a voyage of such length under such confined conditions without one or more members of the expedition finding some excuse to leave it before its termination. Actually we all ended up the best of friends, and throughout our entire voyage there were no quarrels.

Bermuda is a most beautiful spot, and to add to the attractions of the place during our stay were the presence of several warships, among which were the cruisers *Norfolk*, *Dragon* and *Danae*; and the sloop *Dundee*. *Tai-Mo-Shan* did not lie idle, for the waters here are delightful for sailing, and on several occasions officers and their wives came out sailing in her. On one such afternoon we noticed that our topmast had developed a distinct wobble, and as we did not wish to alarm our female guests we did not mention it to them, though we decided to take steps about it before crossing the Atlantic. For this purpose we went to the dockyard and contracted with the staff for the removal of our mainmast for examination. This revealed that the mast had worn unevenly, owing to the stress of the stays, which were shackled to a collar at this point. The addition of an extra sleeve rectified the trouble, but we were not expecting further expense, and the cost of these repairs reduced our funds to a minimum.

We spent a very restful time in the gardens of Admiralty House, which lies on the opposite side of the harbour to the dockyard. Bathing here was grand. The water is a lovely green colour, due to the coral, and there are a variety of bays and sandy beaches which form excellent spots for picnics. Numbers of visitors arrive from New York, a regular service of fast and luxurious liners running regularly between there and this lovely island. The country presents as green an appearance as that of rural England. The houses have white roofs which serve to collect the water, which is an important commodity on an island which has grown up on a reef standing all alone in this vast ocean. When the love of sailing in small boats takes us away on the open sea again, Bermuda will be included in our itinerary.

One evening the Admiral kindly consented to have his family photographed at their house. Our regular photographer being in hospital, another member of the crew went there, armed with the camera and flashlight bulbs. His skill at operating the latter was considerably less than his enthusiasm, and as he was attempting to photograph the evening meal in progress, the consumption of food became a rather difficult matter. Even the Admiral's stewards, who were stationed at the light-switches, were quite unable to control their mirth, for every bulb flashed at the wrong time, and no " shots " were obtained before the supply had run out.

After a month of great enjoyment, of the treatment which the Navy had given us, our sick member was once more in good health, and though we did so with regret, we decided to sail for England without delay. My diary will give a fair description of this final passage across the Atlantic.

CHAPTER XIX

Our Atlantic Crossing

My diary records as follows :

" *Tuesday, 1st May.*

At Sea.   Bermuda to Dartmouth.

"What a wonderful month that was !

"We left this morning at 10 a.m. and were towed out by a dockyard tug, as the wind was most unfavourable for sailing through the narrow channels which intersect the numerous reefs.   We had a great send-off from the officers and ship's company of H.M.S. *Norfolk*, while the Admiral and his family escorted us out in his barge.   When we were out of the dockyard basin and had shouted our farewells to H.M.S. *Norfolk*, H.M.S. *Dragon* and H.M.S. *Dundee*, we passed close to H.M.S. *Danae*, whose officers and men had looked after us so well at Jamaica, and who were now isolated from the other ships owing to an outbreak of German measles. The band and the cheering gave us a big thrill.   When we arrived off Saint George's, the Royal Engineers were flying an international code signal wishing us *Bon Voyage*.   It was there that we slipped the tug and proceeded to hoist our sails.   The tug's captain blew his siren excitedly, and he and his black crew waved us goodbye.   Then we realised we were off : England next stop.

" *Wednesday, 2nd May.*

" All yesterday afternoon I felt miserably ill, and, in fact, was very sick on several occasions. Philip kept me company, while the others, not actually sick, admitted to feeling rotten. The wind is east, and we are sailing north-east by east and doing quite a good speed. It's a bumpy motion and I loathe it !

" Up to noon to-day—113 miles—quite a good start ! We win a dinner if we do it in under thirty days. It is about 3,000 miles.

" I got the officers' cook of H.M.S. *Norfolk* to roast a fowl for me before leaving yesterday, but everybody was so rotten last night, we could not make use of it. However, by this evening we were able to enjoy it with vegetables from Admiralty House. I am not feeling any too certain of myself yet ; the motion is still pretty bad, but to-day I have not actually been ill, though I've felt it—so we are advancing !

" Those chaps in the *Norfolk* were a cheery lot. They would be laughing if they could see my change in colour now.

" It is now 10 p.m. and wind is still east and course north-east by east. We are doing about six knots, which is excellent for close-hauled work. Nice clear sky to-night.

" *Thursday, 3rd May.*

" At noon to-day we had registered another 142 miles, and as we have been close-hauled it is jolly good going. The wind is only force 2, and this afternoon it obligingly veered to south-east, so we are now holding our course of E.N.E. and have got up jib, staysail, jib-top, main, mizzen staysail and mizzen. We are now, at 9.30 p.m., still doing a steady six-and-a-half to seven knots with an easy motion. It has been a lovely sunny day. Sighted a skua, tropic-bird, and some stormy petrels, also many violet-hued Portuguese men-of-war. Ate a flying-fish yesterday—excellent ! The tropic-birds are white, with a long tail, and I used to watch them when bathing at Admiralty House, Bermuda. As they flew over one they became a most beautiful jade-green colour, due to the reflection of the sea where it was shallow. Appetites have returned ; we all enjoyed a bumper stew this evening. Great optimism prevails *re* possibility of a twenty-day passage ! This is ideal sailing now ; seven knots, a comparatively easy motion, and the boat quite dry. We are close to the steamer route from the Gulf of Panama to Fastnet. Nothing sighted to-day, but yesterday we spoke a steamer from Panama *en route* to Marseilles.

" *Friday, 4th May.*   9 p.m.

" Wind abeam throughout day, drawing abaft beam in first dog. We were thus enabled to replace jib and staysail by starboard spinnaker, and though wind has fallen light we are averaging about six knots, steering E.×N.½N. with wind S.×W. (stard. quarter). We roll much more with wind on quarter than on beam, though it is wonderful having such marvellous conditions as this. To noon to-day 172 miles. Had two flying-fish for breakfast—wonderful hot sun and clear sky all day. All very optimistic to-day about a fast passage, even to the extent of a swopping of addresses while on leave ! Just getting into Gulf Stream.

" *Saturday*, 5*th May*.   7 p.m.

" Conditions much the same as yesterday, but heavier roll.   Despite northerly course noon shade temperature still seventy degrees Fahrenheit, and very hot in the sun. To noon to-day 162 miles.   Advanced clock one hour to-day.   Gulf Stream set us on about nine miles in nine hours.   Our excellent progress to date probably due to the fact that I found Red sewing a piece of my best and only pyjama suit into the jib-topsail the day before sailing !

" Short-wave set is not working, but on the Marconi set we picked up Iceberg warning from Ice patrol. Nearest one is some 400 miles from our course.

" *Sunday*, 6*th May*.   7 a.m.

" Conditions different this morning—heavy following sea, giving us eight knots throughout the night and still doing so, though now we have reduced sail to main-sail and starboard spinnaker.   We are rolling badly, which makes sleep a more 'moving' affair than usual, but we are all pleased at being able to maintain the speed. Porridge and boiled eggs are the easiest things to do for breakfast.   We are carrying three hundred eggs which originally came from Miami ;   I do not know how or when they arrived on board H.M.S. *Norfolk*, so I guess the hens concerned must have been missing the results of their handiwork for quite a while now.

" 5 p.m.

" Everything down below in a terrible chaos—wet clothes, papers, books and a very-torn spinnaker litter the saloon.   The wind increased all the forenoon, and by 1 p.m. the seas were so mountainous that we had reduced sail to the jib only.   The spinnaker could not stand up to it and got badly torn before we could lower it. I kept the afternoon watch, while the others worked on it. There was very little space between the point where the seas were dead astern and the point where the jib gybed, which made steering very tricky. We took some big ones aboard, and with only the jib up ran before the seas at over six knots. I am wedged in my bunk now to write this. I think we shall have to heave-to before dark. I shall be glad when we have turned round. The wind is about force 8, and I estimate the seas to be about twenty-five feet high. The confounded barograph still seems going down. My bunk is very wet, as a green one shot down the ventilator and apparently quite a big portion of it has come to rest here. My new rubber clothing has kept me marvellously dry. The clatter of rolling objects is very trying ! However, we shall appreciate the rolling all the more when this depression has passed. To noon to-day, 205 miles, our best day's run to date, and a champagne dinner for beating the two-hundred mark.

"11 p.m.

" ' All hands on deck ! '—Hove-to with staysail and mizzen.

"*Monday, 7th May.*　About 4 a.m.

"Just turned the *Hints-for-the-Household* almanac on and read as follows : 'Ice Cream blocks, or bricks, when not required for immediate use, should be wrapped in a thick towel, blanket or other bad conductor of heat.' This is not encouraging !

"Set jib and continued on course. Weather still looks very threatening and fairly heavy seas are still running. Everything is very damp below. Made cocoa and turned in again.

"About 6 a.m.

"Set mainsail. Rolling a lot. Busy getting ready sausages and mash for breakfast. Barometer is just being obstinate : 30.25.

"10 a.m.

"Down mainsail again ; blowing harder than ever. To noon to-day, 141 miles.

"1 p.m.

"Decided we must heave-to (thank goodness we did !). 'All hands !' Just while preparing for the manœuvre, a huge sea caught us green, filled the cockpit, and George, who was standing on the mizzen rigging, and therefore some four or five feet above the deck, was very shaken as he received it in the pit of the stomach. Luckily he is still with us. She heaves-to well by lashing staysail aback, putting helm over and hoisting reefed mizzen. We were feeling rather relieved that this manœuvre was over when it blew harder than I have ever experienced it before. I tried to measure it with the air-meter, but it has got damaged by salt water, and the others were disgusted when I told them that the result of my labours gave a wind of forty-six miles per hour. Actually it was about twice that speed. When the worst of the storm was over, we took the precaution of binding on storm jib and storm mizzen ready for hoisting, should either the staysail or mizzen carry away. That is the position now, at 4.30 p.m., and it is blowing about force 8, low visibility and some pretty whacking seas, which now and again lift us up and plant us rather rudely on our side.

H

" After the blow just now we were reminded of a re-mark made by Ah Lung, who made our sails for us at Hong Kong. At the time, the question of some rather inferior canvas was being discussed, and Ah Lung indignantly interposed with : ' All can-do for play-pid-gin harbourside, no can-do outside ! ' So at this moment do our thoughts go out to Ah Lung. Our sails, to date, are standing up to it well.

" The barograph is the cynosure of all eyes, but is not going up yet. I am off to my bunk. Peace reigns in the boat except for the swishing of water on the decks of the galley and the creaking of woodwork.

" *Tuesday, 8th May.*   10 a.m.

" It is a week ago since we left Bermuda ; despite this hold-up we have not managed so badly. It is blowing about force 7-8 now, and, though the seas are smaller, there is no sign of a rise of barometer. We were hove-to all night and are now only too eager to get going again. The trouble lies in the strength and suddenness of these squalls, which might cause us to ' broach-to,' so for the present we have no option but to remain just where we are.

" Noon.

" Under way again—heavy rolling but barometer is going up very slowly. Seventy-nine miles to noon. We were hoping to keep up an average of 150 miles a day, and so do the trip in twenty days.

" 4.30 p.m.

" The depression has passed and we now have bright sunshine and a good southerly breeze. Great optimism once more.

" *Wednesday, 9th May.* 7 p.m.

" The wind has been blowing force 4-5 steadily since last night, so we are getting along splendidly, and when we found that up to noon to-day we had done our best day's run—208 miles—we were delighted. The Gulf Stream is helping us along well, but I think we will find a decrease from now on. Glorious sunshine to-day.— Airing bedding, etc.

" Air Temp. at noon 66° F., sea 64°, wind S.S.W. and course E. by N. Barometer is steady.

" *Thursday, 10th May.* 9 a.m.

" Another wonderful morning—bright sunshine— wind S.×E., cse. E.×N.$\frac{1}{2}$N. and logging eight knots, though I think we shall find that this log over-reads. We lost the other one in the gale—also our life-buoy with ' *Tai-Mo-Shan*, Royal Hong Kong Yacht Club ' inscribed on it. I hope the latter is not picked up, but as we have not sighted a ship since the first day out, I do not think this is likely.

" A squid was found on the deck of the galley this morning, having got down the hatch in some peculiar way. If we do twenty-nine miles from eight to twelve this forenoon we beat the 200-mark again. It is en- couraging.

" 9 p.m.

" We just beat the 200-mark, and so I had to produce our one and only chicken, which I had promised them if we did so. Not a cloud in the sky all day, and wind so light that I am afraid our average will be much lower at noon to-morrow. To-night we sighted a ship just at dusk, coming up astern. By the time that she was within signalling distance it was dark. We had a long conversation for which she closed us, promising to report sighting us to Lloyd's and giving us a position which closely coincided with our own results. She was a Frenchman bound for Liverpool ; she finally wished us ' Good Travels and Compliments.' It is a pity that the wind has fallen so light, for earlier in the day we would have been keeping up with her. We are half-way across the Atlantic to-night—little did we expect this marvellous weather, but I cannot help feeling that we are due for another gale soon. Our last chicken was excellent ; I have a turkey up my sleeve, but shall hang on until the weather gets colder.

" *Friday*, 11th *May*.   7.30 p.m.

" Had anyone told me before we started that we would be experiencing absolute calm now, I should have had the greatest difficulty in believing them. Yet such is the case. In fact, I have just had a swim and not a movement on the boat. The sea was pretty fresh and full of tiny jellyfish. There has not been a cloud in the sky all day, and this afternoon was baking-hot.

" By noon we had done 120 miles in the twenty-four hours, and this leaves us with forty-five miles in hand on a daily average of 150. But there is no sign of wind yet, and that in one of the world's biggest gale areas. We are all feeling furious !

" *Saturday*, 12th *May*.   9 p.m.

" Nearly stationary all day. Swam before breakfast and again in the dog watches. We got a violet-coloured Portuguese man-of-war on board in a bucket. They have beautiful colouring on their thread-like tentacles, from which, incidentally, Philip got stung. My book on these subjects says : ' Its stings can have most unpleasant though not necessarily fatal results.' Though I have just read this out, it does not seem to have worried P., who has promptly turned over and gone to sleep. We are getting a little wind now, but all to-day there has been a cloudless sky again, sea like a mill-pond and a hot sun. At any other time, ideal, but not at all what we want for a fast passage. Up to noon to-day, forty-two miles (twenty-four by current). Sighted another ship in the middle watch last night, but too far away for signalling purposes ; that makes the third.

" Turkey, for supper.

" *Sunday*, 13*th May*. 9 p.m.

" More wind to-day, but from East, which is just where we want to get to. Our course now is about North-east, and we are waiting for the wind to veer. It is very cold and it seems extraordinary to think that we were bathing over the side and enjoying a hot sun yesterday. I am afraid that we cannot possibly do the trip under twenty-three or four days now. To noon to-day, forty-one miles, with a set against us of twelve.

" *Monday*, 14*th May*. a.m.

" We had four Rorqual whales in close proximity yesterday, the nearest being about twenty yards off the bow. Fascinating to watch at close quarters, but no one was brave enough to make use of our harpoon. I find in a book that there are ' Flying Squids ' which are believed to fly tail first, which seems to explain the presence of the one on the galley deck.

" I wish the officers' cook of H.M.S. *Norfolk* could see the bread that he made for us. The few remaining loaves are deep green on the outside, but by cutting off the crusts, doing a bit of ' tidying-up ' with the point of a knife, and applying a little butter in these spots, bread is still on the menu. I think that to-morrow, their fifteenth birthday, will see the last of them. We went about at midnight—wind this morning about East, course S.E.×S. Curse this delay ; after nine days' sailing we had done over half the distance, and now our daily runs are below fifty.

" p.m.

" The wind has held East all day, so we have no option but to steer North-east or South-east. It really is getting sickening. At times it falls very light. To noon to-day, forty-nine miles.

" *Tuesday*, 15th *May*. 6 a.m.

" It is a fortnight to-day since we left Bermuda. At the moment I am sitting on the cabin roof ; there is absolute silence down below except for the gurgle of water in the ready-use tank, while, up here, there is no wind. The slatting of the sails almost gives relief to what would otherwise prove a maddening stillness. It is overcast and there is an oily swell. We have finished our stock of bread, but we have loads of biscuits left.

" 11 p.m.

" Moved a little now and again throughout to-day, but now becalmed again. It really is incredible and most depressing. Just now we spoke the ss. *Chagres*, a British steamer. Barometer still remains steady. To noon to-day, twenty-two miles ! !

" *Wednesday*, 16th May.   9 a.m.

" Flat calm again.   However, boredom somewhat relieved by sighting a steamer at 7 a.m. which came up close, the Captain shouting from the bridge.   It was very exciting at the time.   She was the ss. *Montgomery Castle* of New York ;   this makes the fifth.

" 10 p.m.

" We have now got a fresh breeze on the starboard quarter.   With spinnaker, main and mizzen, we are now doing seven knots, which is most encouraging.   To noon to-day, sixty-four miles.

" *Thursday*, 17th May.   a.m.

" We had to shorten sail at midnight, lowering both spinnaker and mizzen, but even so we kept up seven and a half knots.   It was a most boisterous motion which made sleeping very difficult.   It could be achieved a little by lying on one's side in the centre of the bunk and wedging oneself there with every available article of clothing.

" *Friday*, 18th May.

" We have been bowling along at about six knots all to-day, but to-night the wind suddenly slipped round from astern to ahead and has now fallen light.   Slight rain-showers.   Under 1,000 miles to do.   To noon to-day 168 miles.

" *Saturday*, 19th May.

" Practically becalmed throughout last night, but at 8 a.m. the wind freshened and has continued to do so all to-day.   We are now whistling along before a sea on the starboard quarter which is giving us a heavy roll but a satisfactory steady eight knots. If it holds it should only be a matter of a few days to complete the 824 miles to Dartmouth which we had left to do at noon to-day. We are steering E.½S., the wind is S.W. force 4, the noon temperature is 60° F. and the B.B.C. is booming forth into the saloon, so we are all feeling fine, except for an orgy of roly-poly pudding which has just finished. To noon—eighty-six miles.

" *Sunday, 20th May.*

" We kept up a good seven knots all last night and we have had a fine sailing breeze all to-day.

" *Wednesday, 23rd May.*

" This is getting a bit too much of a good thing. All the forenoon we had light head winds. Up to noon, forty-two miles. We want to steer to N.E., but can only achieve N.E. × N. or S.E. × S. Our forenoon was brightened by the visit of a whimbrel, a member of the curlew family, whom he much resembles, but the former can be distinguished by the white band on the head. He is probably *en route* from East Africa to the Western Hebrides, where they go to breed. He was obviously in a bad way on arrival, and now he has certainly not got his sea-legs. He is a most comic sight as he tries to move about the deck. He flew off twice, but was at once attacked by stormy petrels. To-night, after two vain attempts to get hold of him, which ended by him going into the sea, we got him the third time. He is now ensconced up forward in the bosun's store, where he is more likely to survive. Occasionally he supports himself against the roll with his long beak.

" The other incident of note to-day also comes under the Natural History heading : At about 10 a.m. we sighted a shark right close up under the stern. We were able to gauge his size accurately and found his head was four foot across, while, his tail coinciding with the log, the length of line streamed gave us his length as forty feet. It was surprising to meet such a large beast not more than three hundred miles from Land's End. He is almost certain to be a Basking Shark, which are known to attain this length.

" *Sunday, 27th May.* 3 p.m.

" Wind has persisted in remaining easterly, so, at 10 a.m., when nearing Ushant, we went about. We saw several ships about this time. One, the ss. *Brighton*, passed close to us. We are now steering N.¼W., which will about bring us up to Bishop Rock light (Scilly Islands). We want the wind to back or veer considerably before we can lay our course for Dartmouth. To noon to-day, ninety-seven miles. Eggs are still holding out, though some of us prefer to go without !

" *Monday, 28th May.* 9 p.m.

" Head winds have been opposing us all day, but we are now abeam of Bishop Rock light. We have another thirty-five miles to the Lizard. We are all getting very excited, but are longing for this wind to veer. To noon, 104 miles.

" *Tuesday, 29th May.*

" We have just got to the Lizard. Slight fog and light head winds. We are all destroying clothes (some of them have needed it for a long time). Tried to signal the Lizard, but could get no answer from them.

" *Wednesday, 30th May.*   3 p.m.

" I am too excited to make a very intelligent entry. We stood out from the shore during the night, and beat in again this forenoon. We made our landfall near Salcombe, and so did not sight the Eddystone. We are now beating up to Dartmouth. The English country is a refreshing sight."

Tai-Mo-Shan arrived off Dartmouth at eight-thirty that evening, and we were accorded a great reception by the staff and cadets of the Royal Naval College. A motor-boat towed us up the pretty little harbour between two long lines of pulling boats manned by naval cadets. So our voyage came to an end one day under a year from our date of departure from Hong Kong. The crossing of the Atlantic had taken twenty-nine days, adding a final 3,179 miles to our total. The mileage for the entire voyage totalled 16,217½ miles.

Amidst the excitement of our arrival no message of welcome among the many received was more appreciated than this one :

" H.M. the King wishes to welcome the officers of *Tai-Mo-Shan* on their safe arrival home after their eventful voyage from China."

APPENDIX I

Ketch *Tai-Mo-Shan* 20 Tons
Cruising Hong Kong to Dartmouth.

Voyage		Dates	Distance (miles)	Average daily run (miles)
Hong-Kong	to Keelung	1- 6-33— 6- 6-33	545	101
Keelung	,, Yokohama	9- 6-33—20- 6-33	1,144	95
Yokohama	,, Nemuro	2- 7-33—10 -7-33	680	80
Nemuro	,, Attu	14- 7-33—30 7-33·	1,354	74
Attu	,, Unalaska	10- 8-33—17- 8-33	757	118
Unalaska	,, Victoria	23- 8-33—12- 9-33	1,732·5	86·5
Victoria	,, San Francisco	28- 9-33— 7-10-33	819	87·5
San Francisco	,, San Pedro	16-10-33—22-10-33	371	55
San Pedro	,, Acapulco	2-11-33—26-11-33	1,531	57·7
Acapulco	,, La Libertad	6-12-33—13-12-33	691	68·2
La Libertad	,, Panama	16-12-33— 5- 1-34	855	41·6
Panama	,, Jamaica	18- 1-34—26- 1-34	755	90
Jamaica	,, Little Inagua	3- 2-34— 9- 2-34	392	58
Little Inagua	,, Crooked Island	10- 2-34—11- 2-34	146	97·3
Crooked Island	,, Nassau	28- 2-34— 2- 3-34	279	120·8
Nassau	,, Bermuda	23- 3-34— 1- 4-34	987	108·2
Bermuda	,, Dartmouth	2- 5-34—30- 5-34	3,179	109·6
		TOTAL	16,217·5	

CREW :

Lieutenant-Commander M. B. Sherwood,
Lieutenant R. E. D. Ryder   Lieutenant P. S. Francis.
Lieutenant G. S. Salt.   Surgeon Lieutenant C.
Ommaney-Davis.

REMARKS :

From 2nd–7th September on passage from DUTCH HARBOUR to VICTORIA, B.C., covered 826 miles. Daily average, 165 for five consecutive days.

For the first nine days out from BERMUDA, *i.e.* 1–5–34 —10–5–34 distance covered was 1,426 miles. Daily average 158 for nine consecutive days.

BEST DAY'S RUN in Pacific—196 miles (Formosa Channel).

BEST DAY'S RUNS in Atlantic—205 miles (6th May), 208 (9th), 204 (10th).

TAI-MO-SHAN

On a seven-ton Lead Keel with a displacement of 23½ tons, the *Tai-Mo-Shan* is 54 feet over-all and 42 feet designed water-line. Her draft is 8 feet 5 inches and she has a Sail Area of 1,040 square feet in Ketch rig. Her extreme beam is 12 feet 2½ inches, with a beam on the water-line of 10 feet 11½ inches. There is no bow-sprit.

The masts are built of China Fir with the top twelve feet of the mainmast hollow. The hull is teak-planked, and built on camphor and ipol steamed-frames on a teak keel with a yacal stern post and a camphor-wood stem in one piece.

Her construction is slightly in excess of Lloyd's re-quirements. All fastenings are of non-ferrous metal and all floors, hanging knees and chain plates are of steel galvanised after all the fittings had been completed. In order to reduce weight above the water-line the decks are of pine-wood.

For the ½ h.p. motor for charging batteries for the wireless and lighting, petrol is carried in two tanks fitted outside the coach roof and draining outboard.

Three anchors and seventy-five fathoms of half-inch chain are carried, also canvas sea-anchors.

INTERIOR FITTINGS

The interior is fitted with stores forward and a drying-compartment at the forward end of the main saloon, which contains four bunks for the sleeping accommodation. Provisions can be stowed under all the seat lockers, as well as in the cupboards provided for the purpose.

The galley is on the port side of the companion-way, aft of which is the wireless-room, and the chart-room is still further aft on the starboard side. The navigator's bunk is on the port side. The under-water body of the yacht is covered with muntz metal sheeting.

APPENDIX II

Provisions

The one thing that is important on a long ocean voyage is the feeding. There may be times when the thought of food is positively nauseating, but luckily these periods are of short duration. With a party of young fellows with good appetites sound meals add to the contentment of the crew, and undoubtedly prevent any feeling of irritation which might otherwise assert itself after a week or two at sea.

The voyage of *Tai-Mo-Shan* was carefully thought out in this respect, and the following remarks on food are the result of the experience gained on that ship.

And last, but not least, do not forget the tin-opener !

This is a list of stores intended for five people for 100 days, fresh provisions being bought as occasion offers, and with no ice-chest or refrigerator fitted on board.

		REMARKS
FLOUR	150 lbs.	Keeps indefinitely in tin with tight lid. Use for thickening soups ; also in puddings.
SUGAR	100 lbs. (granulated)	Keeps indefinitely in tin with tight lid.
TEA	20 lbs.	
COFFEE	30 lbs.	Preferably ground and in tins.

REMARKS

COCOA	50 lbs.	In tins.
JAMS	30 lbs.	,,
PICKLES	12 bottles	Glass bottles—these can be used for other purposes when empty.
TINNED MEATS	100 lbs.	Fine assortment can be bought nowadays.
SAUSAGES	70 lbs.	In tins.
SALMON	30 lbs.	,,
SARDINES	70 tins	
GOLDEN SYRUP	40 lbs.	This may seem a large quantity but proved very popular in *Tai-Mo-Shan*.
MUSTARD	4 ,,	In tins.
PEPPER	2 ,,	,,
SALT	20 ,,	,,
VINEGAR	4 pints	In wicker-covered jar.
SUET	20 lbs.	In tins—Suet Puddings easy to make and filling.
DRIED PEAS	15 ,,	In tins with tight lid to prevent weevils, etc.
HARICOT BEANS	15 ,,	No need to soak if cooked in Pressure Cooker. Excellent for thick soups.
SPLIT PEAS	15 ,,	
CURRANTS	15 ,,	Keep tin covered and wash before use.
SULTANAS	15 ,,	Keep tin covered and wash before use.
RICE	30 ,,	Tin or sack, but wash before use.
TOMATOES	20 tins	Tomatoes retain their vitamins even when tinned.

REMARKS

SEA BISCUITS	100 lbs.	Each tin to contain about 7½ lbs. If more they will get stale before tin is emptied.
MARMALADE	20 ,,	
TINNED MILK	70 tins	During dark hours, easier than powdered variety.
POWDERED MILK	20 tins (2½ lb. tin)	We used " Klim," which was undistinguishable from the real article.
BACON BELLIES	10 lbs. (if liked)	Packed in salt.
BUTTER	60 tins	1-lb. tins advised—Sample before purchasing, to ensure it is not of the salty variety.
BAKING POWDER	2 ,,	If cooking puddings, which is well worth while.
KRAFT CHEESE	50 ,, (½ lb. tin)	Quick meal in really rough weather.
CHUTNEY	2 bottles	Curries proved very popular in cold and wet weather.
CLOVES	¼ lb.	If liked with apples.
CORNFLOUR	2 lbs.	In tins.
CUSTARD POWDER	10 tins (1-lb. tin)	Popular with tinned fruits —is good made with " Klim."
MIXED DRIED FRUITS	10 lbs.	
DRIED PRUNES	10 ,,	If cooked in Pressure Cooker, no need to soak overnight.
SPAGHETTI	15 ,,	Easily cooked ; don't be stingy with the butter.

REMARKS

FRYING OIL	(8 tins) 5 gal.	Same lot can be used frequently.
DRIED MINT	1 small bottle	With pea-soup adds to the cook's prestige.
NUTMEG	1 small bottle	Useful for flavouring puddings.
VANILLA ESSENCE	1 small bottle	Useful for flavouring puddings.
TINNED FRUITS	72 tins	Always popular and save the cook trouble.
QUAKER OATS (quick)	30 „	Add to boiling water in small quantities. Sufficient for 5 takes few minutes.
SAUCE	15 bottles	Useful for stews.
CARROTS	10 tins	For use when fresh supply finished.
TINNED VEGETABLES	50 „	For use when fresh supply finished.
BOVRIL or MARMITE	15 bottles	Improves stews no end.
BACON AND BEANS	20 tins	Dried variety cooked in Pressure Cooker, with tomato-sauce added are just as good and cheaper.
TINNED SOUPS	as required.	These tins hold so little that it is advisable to use dried peas, beans, lentils, etc., for soups.
CURRY POWDER	1 bottle	Curries recommended.
BISQUICK (or similar article)	12 cartons	This is a quick flour for making scones, etc. No yeast required and simple to manipulate.
EGGS	600	If greased will keep indefinitely without bursting.

REMARKS

POTATOES	2 sacks	Will keep for weeks if kept in dry place and sorted occasionally.
ONIONS	2 ,,	Will keep for weeks if kept in dry place and sorted occasionally.
ORANGES	1 case (200)	Will keep for 2 or 3 weeks away from wet.
CARROTS	1 small sack	Will keep for 2 or 3 weeks away from wet.
FRESH VEGETABLES		Get sufficient for 2-3 days after leaving harbour.
BREADCRUMBS	1 tin	These add to the cook's prestige.

MISCELLANEOUS HINTS

PORPOISE. Can be procured with a harpoon-gun. Steaks are good and liver excellent (if you know where to find it !)

PUFFINS. These birds make excellent stews. Impossible to pluck ; cut feathers around neck and peel plumage off body.

TURTLES. Thrash steaks well with rolling-pin or other suitable article. Excellent eating. Breast-plate, which can be cut up easily, makes best soup. Mind the flippers, as they work for some time after death.

Capture by steering alongside and turning them over with pole.

FISH. Examine all tropical fish carefully when cleaning them. A great number of the Pacific fish are diseased. If doubtful about any fish, insert a piece of silver and boil with a piece of the fish. If latter is poisonous, silver will be tarnished.

PLUCKING BIRDS. To pluck birds, first place body in bucket of warm water and feathers can then be easily removed.

PEELING ONIONS. To prevent " tears " cut the " root " end first.

WASHING-UP. All hands should take turns at this necessary evil. A great deal of labour can be saved by eating all courses out of an enamel bowl.

REMOVAL OF GREASE. Newspapers etc. are good for removing grease and save the dish-cloth.

GLASSES. Unbreakable tumblers are highly recommended.

UPPER DECK

Our final cooking arrangements after practical experience had been gained were as follows : We had a simple double-burner gas-ring, suspended from the deck above by an iron bracket at the after end and fitting into a recess in the bulkhead at the for'd end. This arrangement was in my opinion an excellent one and very simple at the same time. A flexible rubber pipe joined on to the supply tube and connected the gas-ring to two cylinders of " Rock Gas." This is a gas bottled under pressure, which we purchased in British Columbia. It burned with an exceedingly hot flame and was practically odourless. I can thoroughly recommend this type of gas for use in yachts. I think that something akin to it can be purchased in England.

A ring was placed around one burner to fit our pressure-cooker, while a portable oven[1] could be used for baking on the other burner. We did not have a sink, which was a mistake, and its absence entailed a great deal of extra work filling and emptying buckets.

[1] Portable ovens can be purchased for a few shillings at any hardware store.

Overhead was a five-gallon ready-use fresh-water tank, which was supplied by a hand-pump from the main tanks.

PRESSURE COOKERS

We purchased a British-made pressure-cooker called the "Pentecon." It proved to be absolutely invaluable. Not only did it cook well but it saved tremendous time and labour. Incidentally so little water does it require that it also effected a great saving of this precious commodity. The chief advantage, however, was the fact that the steam-pressure made it impossible for the cover to be removed during the cooking process, and consequently no mess could result. Indeed on more than one occasion when we were rolling heavily, the Pentecon was bottom-up on the deck, with no evil effects. I certainly would not proceed on a long voyage without one of these excellent articles had I to practise the culinary art again. The book of recipes supplied made good cooking a very much easier task than I had anticipated.

ARTICLES FOR THE GALLEY.

Do not forget these articles in addition to knives, spoons, forks, etc.

> Mincing machine.
> Knife-sharpener
> Rolling-pin.　(Can be used for defence purposes when the victims don't like the victuals !)
> Corkscrews.
> Bottle-openers.
> 1 pair fish scissors.

SOME SIMPLE RECIPES WHICH PRODUCE THE GOODS.

POTATO DOUGHNUTS

1 cup mashed-potatoes.
1 tablespoon butter.
1 cup granulated sugar.
1 cup milk.
1 teaspoon lemon extract } Not essential—use a little nutmeg if you
1 teaspoon vanilla } have it.
½ teaspoon salt.
2 heaping teaspoons baking-powder.
Flour enough to make a very soft dough.
3 eggs beaten.

Mix all the above together well and roll out flat till about 1½" high.

Cut doughnuts out (use lid of a tin).

Cut out small hole in centre of each.

Fry in deep fat and sprinkle with sugar.

CLAM CHOWDER

Boil 1 quart of milk with pepper.

Melt 2 tablespoons butter and mix with 2 heaped tablespoons of flour.

Thin with some of the milk—then pour into milk, stirring constantly.

Boil together 1 onion chopped, 1 carrot grated, and 1 potato. Fry 6 rashers bacon and cut into bits.

Put the lot into the milk and add tin of clams.

Flavour with Worcester Sauce and salt.

PASTRY

(This is not nearly so difficult as the experts would have it.)

1 cup flour, ⅛ teaspoonful of salt, pinch of cream of tartar. (Cream of tartar can be dispensed with if you have not got any.)

Put into the above ½ cup of lard, butter or shortening, then add just enough cold water to make it hold together. Roll out (not more than once, if possible, or it will be tough). Place on top of pie-dish, decorate with knife, and cut an air-hole in the top of the pie-crust, to let the steam escape.

BREAD-MAKING

(With yeast, for 5 people for about 3 days.)

Take 10 lbs. flour ; mix up 3 lbs. flour and 2 oz. yeast—little warm water (say 2 pints). Put in warm place—allow to rise—takes about ½ hour.

After this period, take water (cold water in hot climate, and vice versa), 4-5 oz. salt, and mix all up together = 7 + 3 lbs. Then put in warm place and allow to rise again for approximately ½-hour.

After ½-hour, place in mould and when about double height of mould, put in stove ; slow bake.

PANCAKES—5 people

Take 1 lb. flour, 5 eggs, little salt, 2 oz. sugar. Mix together and add milk in slowly—not all at once. Add spoonful of melted butter and mix well. Melt some butter in the pan. Put in 4-5 tablespoonfuls of the mixture ; when half-baked, toss up and over.

SWEET OMELETTE—5 people

2 small ones best.

Take 8 eggs for each omelette, break and add sugar and little salt. Stir up. Test with finger for sweetness. Put butter in pan, heat and put mixture in. Stir with fork, add jam. Turn edges over when setting.

ORDINARY OMELETTE—No Sugar.

CORNMEAL BREAD
(Highly recommended)

1½ cups flour.
1 cup cornmeal.
5 teaspoonfuls baking powder.
1   „   salt.
2   „   sugar.
2 tablespoons lard
1   „   butter.
2 eggs.
2 cups of milk.

Put flour, cornmeal, baking powder, sugar, salt, all in together and mix well.

Add lard and butter, and use your fingers to mix it in well. (If using paraffin-stoves, it is advisable to wash the hands first.)

Add 2 beaten eggs and 2 cups of milk.

If the mixture is a little too dry, add a little water. Put in baking-dish and bake in hot oven. It should only take about 15 minutes.

The cost per head of food for the entire voyage of *Tai-Mo-Shan*—364 days—came to twenty pounds.

APPENDIX III

Ocean Winds

In the first place, the *Sailing Directions*, excellent volumes that they may be, and compiled by the most competent sailing-ship masters of the past, can scarcely be called encouraging to those who navigate in small vessels, and it is probable that if they had been produced in time nobody would have been foolish enough to put to sea at all. Pilot charts and wind atlases give you the bare facts and statistics, and are the chief guide in planning a voyage. People approach this matter, as far as one can see, from two different aspects. Either they want to visit a particular part of the world, or else they merely wish to sail where the going is easiest.

In *Tai-Mo-Shan* the course that we took was decided on because we wanted to visit the Aleutian Islands, and the winds had to be worked out accordingly. With unlimited time at one's disposal much easier sailing routes can be chosen. But, instead of having continually to work round the Trade Wind areas, one can run down wind. The design of the boat and equipment will be a deciding factor. A steady stream of yachts of all sizes and shapes leave England annually and run down-wind and are to be found in the West Indies, from whence they can continue their voyage through the Canal and down to the South Sea Islands.

Let me assume that one is going to a specific place and

wishes to find the best route to get there. The first thing to look for is the percentage of gales and of calms. We found that a percentage of gales over 18 per cent. was not good going, and anything over 30 per cent. calms brought our daily average down to about fifty miles. In the voyage of *Tai-Mo-Shan* across the North Pacific and North Atlantic we sailed a northerly course in the summer and a southerly one in the winter. This was more by force of circumstances than by intention. The average force of wind experienced in the Pacific was a meagre 1·47 on the Beaufort scale and our average up to Panama was only seventy-five miles a day. In order to navigate the globe east about one must keep in fairly high latitudes to hold the Variables or Westerlies. These winds are formed by the continual passing of depressions further to the north and the course should be planned as far as possible to ensure keeping to the equator side of them.

In the Northern Hemisphere the wind will then start in the south and work round through south-west to west. If one can press home hard enough it may be possible to keep up with the passage of these depressions and make excellent passage. If, as frequently happens, one is forced to heave-to, or one's ship is not fast enough, they come and go so quickly that one is apt to be left chafing in the calms between.

With regard to calms these are most persistent in or near the areas of high pressure or anticyclones such as those that cover the Azores in summer. The best wind for passage-making in a yacht like *Tai-Mo-Shan* is force 5 abeam or force 7 astern.

Certain areas of calms, and one thinks with feeling of

the Pacific coasts of Lower California, Mexico and Central America can be sailed through slowly by making use of the land and sea breezes which, being local winds, are not indicated on the wind charts for those regions. They blow at certain times of the year with great regularity, and we found ourselves gybing regularly before settling down to the evening meal etc. in readiness for the land breeze on which we could depend. The latter blows from about 2,200 to sunrise and the sea-breeze from about 1,400 to about 1,900, neither probably attaining more than force 1-2. They will be " reaching " winds, and as one will probably do as much as three and a half to four knots one should make about forty-fifty miles a day. So much for the wind-charts ; their use is really commonsense, but as a rough guide thirty per cent. calms can be considered as no wind for practical purposes. With twenty-three per cent. gales, it seems to be blowing very hard most of the time, while with fifty-five per cent. fog, conditions bear a close resemblance to an area of permanent fog.

APPENDIX IV

Remarks on Navigation

These remarks are not intended as a standard work on Navigation ; in fact, an attempt has been made to avoid encroaching on the subjects covered by such excellent works of those of Dr. Worth and the Admiralty Manual of Navigation. It is hoped, however, that these notes may possibly be of use as a supplement to some of these standard works.

LEEWAY. This is only apparent when close-hauled or full and bye. In *Tai-Mo-Shan* the following rough rule was applied.

WIND	SEA	SAIL	PROGRESS	LEEWAY
Fine Weather	Calm	All sail	Good	Nil
Fresh Winds	,,	Four Lowers	,,	¼ point
Strong ,,	Moderate	Jib-Staysail, close-reefed Main and Mizzen	Mod.	½ ,,
Fresh ,,	Mod. or choppy	Four Lowers	Poor	¾ ,,
Strong ,,	Rough Sea	Jib-Staysail, close-reefed Main and Mizzen.	,,	I ,,

This is at the best only an approximation. Leeway is a tricky thing to estimate, but the best line to go on is probably a close consideration of the strength of wind and the corresponding speed through the water. If one considers that the progress is good, the chances are that leeway will be small. When one's speed falls through bouncing into short, choppy sea, leeway mounts up pretty quickly. It is subject to much larger fluctuations in smaller boats than in larger ones.

When hove-to, a deep-draught vessel like *Tai-Mo-Shan* makes about one knot at ninety degrees to the direction of the wind.

ERRORS IN DEAD RECKONING. These are almost entirely due to a wrong estimation of the course steered with the ship "yawing." There is, in fact, nearly always a tendency for the ship to yaw off her course, generally to windward to avoid a gybe. On the other hand, when it becomes necessary to keep putting the ship stern on to the sea, or when trying to carry a spinnaker with a beam wind, there is a tendency to steer to leeward of one's course. With a fresh wind and sea, nearly astern, an allowance of three-quarters of a point to windward was allowed on our trip.

Drifting at low speeds of about one knot, even the best logs will stop registering, or under-register. It then becomes necessary to estimate the speed and obtain the run by time and speed. If this is neglected, after a day or so of calm, quite large errors will be experienced and will probably be attributed to current.

USE OF INSTRUMENTS AND SOME OF THEIR ERRORS

SEXTANT. The chief errors in the use of a sextant in a small vessel are failure to take the angle vertical and failure to take the sight from the top of a sea. To overcome these errors it is best to use the Star telescope always and to put in a small amount of " side error," so that the reflected image overlaps the direct image. It is then easier to sweep the sun or star along the horizon by canting the sextant in the prescribed manner.

After several days of heavy weather it is reasonable to assume that the vessel may be anything up to fifty miles from her D.R. and any sight is better than no sight. With spray coming over and the horizon only visible intermittently, a low-power telescope with cross-wires will be of considerable assistance. It is necessary to prepare the telescope on a calm day and mark it with a scratch on the sliding portion so that it is at once in focus with the cross-wires vertical.

COMPASS.   Vertical iron or steel rods play havoc with the compass in a wooden vessel at a considerable range. The best way of using compasses with confidence is to have two, the standard and the steering being as far as possible apart. The errors will then be to a large extent equal and opposite. In *Tai-Mo-Shan*, although the errors were up to a point on certain courses and the differences between the two compasses as much as twenty degrees, no correcting magnets were used. If the standard compass can be used for taking azimuths, the errors will be gradually ascertained and by means of a graph and comparison with each other, the compasses may be relied on with every confidence.

Magnets are apt not only to lose their magnetism but to increase heeling error, and, though opinions on the subject will differ, we found it best to use no correctors at all.   A hand observer compass, fitted with a flashlight in the handle, made by Hughes and Son of Fenchurch

Street, was found invaluable for coastal work and for the identification of stars at sea.

DIRECTIONAL WIRELESS. One of the greatest boons to the navigator of a small yacht is Directional Wireless. The one in use in *Tai-Mo-Shan* was constructed at sea in under an hour, and did magnificent work. In higher latitudes, where the fog intensity was of high percentage, the value of this instrument cannot be exaggerated. The Frame Coil used was made by bolting two pieces of wood, three feet long, in the form of a cross. At the ends of each were six holes to take six strands of No. 28 Colton wire which were threaded round and brought to two terminals at the lowest point.

This was hung by a hook from a beam on the centre line and connected to the aerial and earth of a four-valve Marconi receiver, capable of working from 150 kilocycles (2,000 metres) to 650 kilocycles (460 metres). A relative bearing could be obtained by marks on the beam, and the ship's course noted at the same time, but if greater accuracy was required the hand observer compass was used.

The use of direction-finding does not entail a knowledge of the Morse Code, and is well within the scope of any yachtsman.

WIRELESS STATION. The details of these are given in *The Admiralty List of Wireless Signals*; they are divided into groups as follows :

(a) W/T D.F. These are of little use to a yachtsman, as it is necessary to transmit and ask them for your bearing, for which there is also a charge.

(b) W/T Beacon. These are the most useful to the amateur, as they transmit a recognisable call sign in slow time for the express purpose of ships wishing to take their own bearings. As a rule they make a clear-weather transmission half-hourly and transmissions in

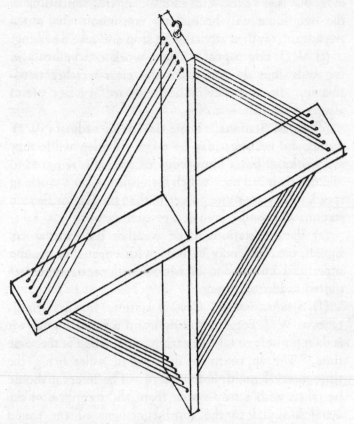

fog continuously. This alone is of value. Take, for instance, a vessel making a landfall on or near Start Point. As frequently happens, the lighthouse is capped in low cloud or fog, while from the deck of a small vessel the visibility is good. Accordingly one carries on in the hope of sighting the light, and may be steering into danger while still thinking oneself to be outside the arc of visibility. With the intelligent use of wireless, however, one is at once aware of the dangerous situation, as the lighthouse will be making continuous fog transmissions. It is then advisable to stop and take a bearing.

(c) W/T Fog Signal. These work continuously in fog only, but do not make the clear-weather transmission. Because they cannot be heard, it is not safe to assume that there is no fog.

(d) Coast Stations. These deal with ordinary W/T traffic, and bearings may be taken of them while they are working, but a knowledge of Morse is required to identify their call sign, which is transmitted at a working speed. They are more powerful than the Fog or Beacon stations and can be used at a greater range.

(e) Various stations make weather bulletins, storm signals, etc., and may be used with effect, but again a superficial knowledge of Morse will probably be required to identify them.

(f) *Synchronisation.* Certain stations make a simultaneous W/T Fog transmission and a sound signal. It is then possible to take a bearing and a range at the same time. The approximate distance in miles being the time interval multiplied by 0.18. The interval should be taken with a stop-watch from the reception of the wireless signal to the commencement of the sound signal. The same may be done with a submarine sound signal ; in this case the interval is multiplied by 0.08.

(g) *Rotating Loop.* At present there appears to be only one, which is at Orfordness, for experimental purposes.

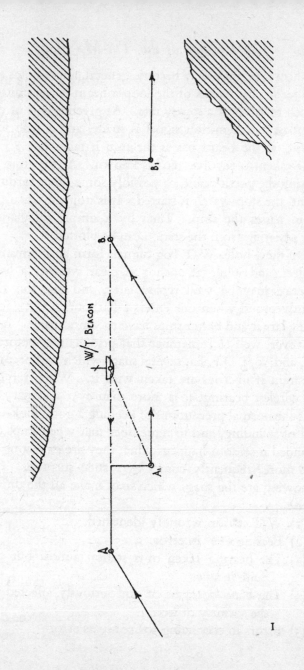

As, however, they may become general, a few notes are included. By means of the loop a beam is transmitted which revolves at a steady rate. At given points of the compass a recognition signal is made, and a dash follows ; as the beam passes the ship it fades out. The time taken to revolve 360° is known. At the time of passing the north point, or possibly some other cardinal point, the stop-watch is started. It is stopped when the beam passes the ship. Then by a simple calculation one's bearing from the station can be plotted.

On the whole, W/T Fog Signals form an interesting subject, and while at anchor in clear weather a little practice may be well repaid later, and one can feel rightly proud when one enters a harbour in thick fog, while larger and better ships have to wait outside. It is, however, well to remember that pride comes before a fall, and W/T D.F. has several snags which will become apparent if liberties are taken with it. When relying on wireless bearing, it is more than ever necessary to take the normal precautions of keeping a good look-out and of sounding, and to remember that when ships are stranded it seldom happens when they are expecting it, but more frequently comes as a rude surprise. The following are the snags which may make all the difference :

(1) W/T station wrongly identified.
(2) Bearing 180° in error.
(3) The bearing taken of a station almost but not quite in line.
(4) The hand compass or coil seriously affected by the vicinity of iron.
(5) Errors in correcting for compass error.

(6) Accumulations of smaller errors due to the well-known causes, such as land effect and the various conditions which render the bearings transmitted as unreliable.

In *Tai-Mo-Shan* we considered the effective maximum range for the set was thirty miles for the beacons and fifty miles for the more powerful stations. The station should be picked up and identified on the main aerial first, probably before it is audible on the frame coil. The lead from the coil to the set should be kept short and the bearings taken of the weakest signals when the coil lies in a plane at right angles to the bearing. A mean should be taken of as many bearings as possible. In the set described, the errors were really surprisingly small and could generally be relied on to a $\frac{1}{4}$ point, if a good selection of them were meaned. A single snap bearing might well be over a point in error.

In certain cases such as light vessels it is possible to use the bearing 180° in error. It is frequently possible to detect this by sailing at right angles to the bearing.

In the figure. If the ship is at *A* and turns on to what she thinks will be a suitable course to pass the light vessel, she may be at *B*. A short alteration of course at right angles, as shown, will soon settle the matter : if the bearing draws to the left, she is at *A*, and if it draws to the right, she will be at *B*.

APPENDIX V

Remarks on Navigation, Sun and Star Sights

This Appendix is an attempt to reduce navigation with a sextant to its simplest terms. The method described is the Dreisenstok Method, and is in common use in America, where it was first produced for use in aircraft. It has many advantages when used in small sailing-vessels, being quick and simple. The quickness is not so important, but the simplicity renders mistakes in the calculations perceptibly fewer and further between.

Required—Dreisenstok Navigation Tables for Use of of Mariners and Aviators. H. 208. The American Nautical Almanac and Chart.

Details for working all sights and examples appear in the beginning of the Tables and once first principles are mastered they can be worked out from these.

The angle observed by the mariner between the sun's lowest edge and the horizon at a particular instant is taken with a sextant ; it is called the altitude ; a stop-watch is started at the same instant and stopped when the chronometer time is noted ; the difference between the chronometer and Greenwich time is known, so that by a simple process of subtraction and addition the Greenwich time at which the altitude was taken is obtained. It is known as G.M.T. Now for the calculations. The mariner must assume that there is a circle on the earth

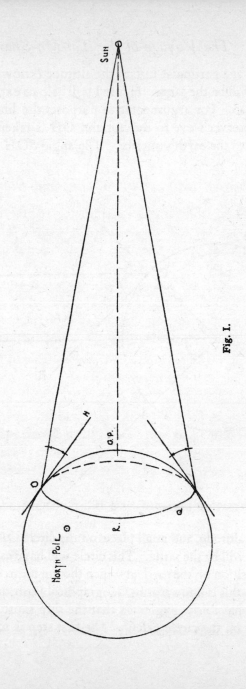

Fig. I.

where at a particular instant the altitude (known as Obs. Alt.) will be the same. Figure I will help to explain why this is so. For argumentative purposes the line joining the observer's eye to the horizon *OH* is taken as tangential to the earth's surface. The angle *SOH* will then

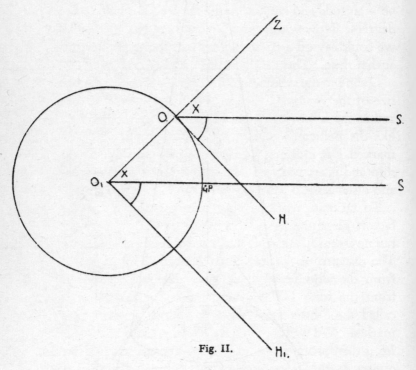

Fig. II.

be the altitude, and at all places on the circle *ORQ* the altitude will be the same. This circle will have as its centre the position on the earth at which the sun is directly overhead—this is known as its Geographical Position, or G.P.

We have now explained that the ship must be somewhere on the circle *ORQ*. The first step is to find the sun's G.P. at the instant of sight. The next will be to calculate the radius of the circle. The G.P. is given in *The Nautical Almanac*.

In Fig. II, the sun being distant, SO is parallel to S_1O_1, so that the angle SOZ equals the angle S_1O_1Z, equals $90° -$ altitude and equals also the arc O.G.P. measured in degrees. Now with centre G.P. and arc ($90° -$ altitude) we could lay off a circle and say that the ship was on it at that time. This is called the Position Circle.

Owing to the smallness of the charts and the enormous size of the Positive Circle, it is not possible to do this, and so the following method is used. Fig. III is a chart like the Bellman's chart, it has no soundings. The $+$ marked DR indicates the approximate position of the ship and is arrived at by laying off the courses steered and distances run from the last fix.

To facilitate working a position C is selected. The factors governing its selection will be dealt with later, but now the D.R. can be dismissed from our calculations. The distance of the ship from the sun's G.P. is found from the altitude $= 90° -$ altitude. The distance of C from the sun's G.P. is calculated. The difference is called the " Intercept." In Fig. III the position C is marked. We want to draw the Position Circle of which PL is the portion required ; it appears as a straight line owing to the magnitude of the circle. The ship is somewhere on the line PL: we hope and assume that it is between P and L, that is to say, reasonably near the DR. To lay off PL—From C draw the Intercept CK towards the direction of the sun or away in the reverse direction, according to circumstances. Draw PL to pass through K and perpendicular to CK.

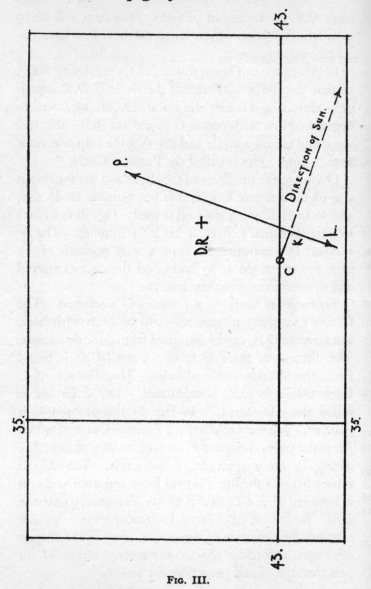

FIG. III.

SAMPLE SIGHT

12th May, 1934. 0800 (Zone + 2) = (1000 Greenwich Time) DR. 43° 05′ N
35° 05′ W

	Chronometer A. 36 mins. 26 secs.	Slow on G.M.T.

		h.	m.	sec.		
A Chron.	-	09	28	00	Obs. Alt. -	31° 28′·5
Stop-watch -		-1	39		Sextant error -	- ·5
Chron. time -	09	26	21			31° 28′·0
Slow - -	+36	26			Correction -	+21′·1
Greenwich time	10	02	47		Time Alt. H₀.	31° 49′·1
(G.M.T.)						

Pick out   Calculated Hc. 31° 46′·5
→from body   Alt.
of table II.

8. G.H.A. Intercept - 2′·6
9. Nautical Almanac 330° 56′·3 towards
   12th May. 1000 094°·7 ←
   G.M.T.
10. Correction for 2
    min. 47 sec. - 41′·8 Declination 18°00′·6 N.

11. Suns G.H.A. - 331° 38′·1
12. Long. of C. - 34° 38′·1

13. t - - - 297° 0′=63° (Supplement) } Enter Table I. ←
14. L. : Lat. of C. - = 43°

15.	Dec. 18° 00′·6 N.			
16.	→b. 25° 57′·5 N.	A. 120 03	C. 186	Z′ 36·8
				(All table I.
17.	43° 58′·1 Table II	B. 158 49	II. D. II. 16	(under t 63)
				(L 43)
18.		+278 52	+ 202	Z″ 57·9
19.				± 94·72 →

KEY TO SAMPLE SIGHT

(a) Work down to G.M.T.

(b) Under G.M.T. 1000, 12th May, look in *Nautical Almanac*, p. 16, under the column Sun's G.H.A.

(c) Against 2 m. and 47 sec. look out the appropriate correction at the end of the sun's information. Add lines 9 and 10 to obtain 11.

(d) The position C is chosen so that (1) It is on a parallel of Latitude nearest to DR; (2) So that G.H.A. minus Longitude gives a complete number of degrees (West Longitude), or so that G.H.A. plus the Longitude gives a complete number of degrees, line 11.

(e) Subtract line 12 from 11 to obtain *t* in line 13.

$$297° = 360° - 297° = 63°.$$

When *t* is between 90° and 270° the supplement is used and the rules for Case II. are applied. Line 14 is the nearest Latitude to DR = 43° N.

(f) With $t = 63°$, $L = 43°$, enter Table I. and take out the whole of line 16.

(g) Line 17 *b*~dec. In Case I. *b* takes the same name as Latitude. In Case II. *b* takes the opposite name to Latitude.

With dec. and *b* *same* names *add*.

" " " opposite " subtract.

(h) With *b*~dec. (43° 58'·1) enter Table II. and take out B and D.

(k) With $A + B$ (278° 52') hunt through Table II. col. hc. and pick out corresponding Hc.

With $D + C$ (202) hunt through Table II. col. *z"* and pick out corresponding *z"*

If $D + C$ exceed 9999 dock off 1000.

(l) In Case I. add *z'* and *z"*. In Case II. *z'* becomes minus. If *b*~dec. exceeds 90° use supplement and give *z"* a negative value.

(m) If Ho is greater than Hc the intercept is towards the bearing *z*. If Ho is less than Hc the intercept is away from the bearing *z*. Great Observed Altitude Towards = GOAT.

(n) Before noon *z* gives true bearing. After noon 360° − *z* gives true bearing.

(o) To obtain Ho apply the sextant error (−·5) to the Observed Altitude. Add correction for height of eye.

NOTE : Instead of using the Calculated Zenith Distance and the Observed Zenith Distance (*i.e.* 90° − altitude), the altitudes are used direct to save working.

APPENDIX VI

Beaufort Wind Scale

Beaufort No.	Nautical M.P.H.	Feet per Sec.	Description
0	Less than 1	Less than 2	Calm
1	1–3	2–5	Light Air
2	4–6	6–11	Light Breeze
3	7–10	12–18	Gentle „
4	11–16	19–27	Moderate ,,
5	17–21	28–36	Fresh „
6	22–27	37–46	Strong „
7	28–33	47–56	Moderate Gale
8	34–40	57–68	Fresh „
9	41–47	69–80	Strong „
10	48–55	81–93	Whole „
11	56–65	94–110	Storm
12	Above 65	Above 110	Hurricane

APPENDIX VII

Dimensions of Various Fittings

These measurements apply to *Tai-Mo-Shan* and will serve as a guide to those designing a vessel of a similar nature :

MAIN HATCH.	2′ 6″ × 2′ 2″.
FORE HATCH.	24″ × 15½″ (Oval).
COCKPIT.	19″ deep × 3′ wide × 3′ long.
COUNTER HATCH.	14½″ diameter.
SALOON TABLE.	2′ 6″ high × 3′ square.
SEATS.	1′ 3″ to 1′ 6″ high.
BUNKBOARDS	10½″ high.
BUNKS.	6′ 3″ long × 2′ 3″ high × 2′ wide (varying slightly).
FOOD LOCKERS.	These totalled 174½ cubic feet and proved ample even when we had embarked 100 days' supply for the five members of the crew.

APPENDIX VIII

Water Supply

In *Tai-Mo-Shan* 250 gallons of water were carried, representing 1.16 tons in weight and occupying approximately forty cubic feet. The distribution was as follows : Six separate tanks holding a total of 226 gallons were situated in the bilges. A twenty-gallon gravity tank was placed overhead in the galley, and a smaller five-gallon tank acted as a subsidiary. A flexible pressure pipe could be connected from the tanks to the pump.

Our allowance was one gallon per day per man, to to include all uses. This was found to be ample and meant that we had a two-months' water-supply.

> 1 gallon of water weighs 10 lbs.
> 1 cubic foot of water weighs 62.8 lbs.
> 1   ,,   ,,   ,,   contains 6.25 gallons.

APPENDIX IX

List of Papers Required by a Sea-going Yacht

	FORM, ETC.	REMARKS
Every Sea-going Yacht.	1. Bill of Sale.	If an old boat, from previous owner.
	2. Builders' Certificate.	If a new boat both 1 and 2 required.
	3. Certificate of Registry.	From Harbour Office.
	4. Certificate of Ownership or Joint Ownership.	From Harbour Office.
Every Yacht visiting Foreign Waters.	5. Bill of Health.	From Local Port Medical Authorities.
	6. Clearance Certificate.	From Harbour Authorities or Customs.
	7. Receipt for Light Dues.	From Harbour Office.
	8. Panama or Suez Canal Certificate.	From Canal Zone or Local Marine Surveyor.
	9. Immigration Papers.	From Consul of country to be visited.
	10 Crew List and Passport.	Passport necessary if travelling inland.
	11. De-ratization and Fumigation Certificates.	Required in some countries. Enquiries should be made.
	12. Admiralty Warrant for Ensign other than RED.	From Admiralty, Whitehall.

APPENDIX X

Medical

In any ocean trip one does not expect to have illness, but minor complaints are bound to arise, while accidents may happen at any time. During the earlier part of the trip of *Tai-Mo-Shan*, sunburn and prickly heat were our only troubles. At sea, cuts and abrasions did not become septic, nor did any of us suffer from common colds. Presumably, fresh air and sunlight killed off any pathogenic bacteria that may have accompanied the yacht as extra passengers from the last port of call. At different times cuts required sutures, and off the coast of Alaska one member of the crew suffered such violent toothache that, although he was not at all sure of the operative abilities in dental surgery of the doctor, he submitted himself as a victim. Under local anaesthesia the tooth was removed quite painlessly and successfully, so much so that at Victoria, when X-rays showed that four more molars must go, he was quite content for the yacht to be the surgery.

During the two weeks which we were forced to spend on the beach at Crooked Island, we were all working very hard and living under most uncomfortable conditions. We received numerous cuts and abrasions on our hands and feet, to which we had no time to give attention. Added to this was the intolerable irritation caused by sandfly and mosquito bites, which resulted in septic sores. When we arrived at Nassau only one of the crew was clear of these troubles ; of the other four, one had a considerable number of boils, two had chronic ulcers on their hands and feet, and the last was unfortunate enough to get some virulent infection through an abrasion which resulted in a cellulitis, necessitating his leg being opened in hospital. The enforced four weeks' stay at Bermuda due to his sickness was enough to put us all in good health again. However, we can hardly blame yachting for these things, and the deep-sea yacht is not liable to meet with them.

The minor things that are likely to occur are constipation, toothache, sunburn, prickly-heat and small abrasions, of which more will be said later.

A complete list of Medical Stores is given, and may be considered excessive, but as one of the crew was a medical man, chloroform, ether and surgical instruments were taken, so that a major operation or an amputation could be performed if necessary. The following is a list of medical stores which are recommended for a yacht undertaking a similar ocean cruise, and is followed by a few first-aid hints on their use and the methods of treatment.

LIST

Bandages—2-inch	24
Boric Lint	1 lb.
Cotton-Wool	1 lb.
Mackintosh Tissue	2 yards
Adhesive Tape	4 yards
Gauze	$\frac{1}{2}$ lb.
Tincture of Iodine	$\frac{1}{2}$ lb.
Horsehair (for sutures) tubes	12

Morphia Ampoules	-	-	-	12	
Syringe with needles	-	-	-	1	
Nikalgin Jelly (for sunburn)			-	1 lb.	
Epsom Salts	-	-	-	1 lb.	
Bicarbonate of Soda	-	-	-	½ lb.	
Aspirin Gr. V tablets	-	-	-	50	
Quinine Sulphate Gr. V tablets			-	50	
Dovers Powder Gr. V tablets			-	50	
Calomel Gr. I tablets			-	50	
Boracic Ointment	-	-	-	4 oz.	
Carbolic Acid (pure)	-	-	-	2 oz.	
Surgical Spirit	-	-	-	1 lb.	
Knife	-	-	-	-	1
Artery Forceps (pair)	-	-	-	1	
Dressing Forceps (pair)		-	-	6	
Scissors (pair)	-	-	-	-	1
Gutta Percha					

Morphia comes under the Dangerous Drugs Act and will necessitate the Captain's signature.

Carbolic Acid is strong and should be carefully stowed and used with caution.

Septic Spots or Abrasions. Treat by hot fomentations. Soak a piece of Boric Lint in boiling water, wring out and apply while hot to the affected part. Cover the lint with a piece of mackintosh tissue to prevent soaking up the bandage ; cover this with cotton-wool and bandage up. Repeat this two or three times a day, until there is no further purulent discharge. Afterwards dress with dry lint until healed.

Burns. Apply a thick layer of Nikalgin Jelly on a piece of gauze and place this on the affected part. Bandage lightly.

Cuts. When a cut extends completely through the skin and the wound gapes, it should be sutured. First scrub the hands and nails well ; clean the wound inside and out with Tincture of Iodine ; next break a tube of horsehair and thread it on to a needle which has been previously boiled for ten minutes. Then, starting at about a quarter of an inch from the edge of the cut, pass the horsehair downwards through the skin on one side and up through the skin on the other side ; cut the horsehair at a convenient length, draw the edges of the wound together and tie with a reef-knot. A long cut may require several sutures like this, and, if such is the case, place them about half an inch apart. Afterwards swab again with Tincture of Iodine and apply a dry gauze dressing secured in position by a bandage or adhesive tape.

Toothache. If the pain is due to a cavity, relief may be obtained temporarily by placing in it a piece of cotton-wool soaked in carbolic acid. This must be done carefully, as a drop of the acid on the gums will cause a painful burn. Next, soften a small piece of gutta percha in a flame and press into the cavity, afterwards smoothing off the edges with the warmed handle of the dressing-forceps.

Broken Bone. Provided the skin is intact, the limb should be splinted to prevent further injury and the patient kept in his bunk until medical assistance can be obtained. If the skin has been broken it is important that antiseptic dressings should be kept on the wound, in addition to the splints. Only when pain is extremely severe should morphia be given.

Method of Administering Morphia. The syringe is assembled with a needle, spirit is drawn up and pumped out several times to sterilise it. Remove plunger and allow a few minutes for it to dry. Next, cut through the neck of one of the ampoules with the file provided, and draw up the contents. Clean an area of the outer part of the arm with spirit or Tincture of Iodine, then push needle through the skin at an angle of fifteen degrees with the surface—inject slowly.

Constipation. Epsom Salts or two grains of Calomel. We also found that the Alophen pills of Parke, Davis and Co were excellent.

Food Poisoning. To get rid of the poison give large doses of salt-water or mustard in water. This will promote vomiting. Afterwards give Epsom Salts.

Sickness or Flatulence. Gastric discomfort can often be cured by giving a teaspoonful of Bicarbonate of Soda in water every three hours.

Sunburn. Smear Nikalgin Jelly on the affected part ; it will give relief rapidly.

Prickly Heat. This is a common complaint in the Tropics ; it is caused by excessive perspiration and is characterised by a rash, appearing usually at the bends of joints. There is a good deal of soreness and tenderness associated with it. Weak carbolic acid usually clears the condition in a few days. The strength of solution is a teaspoonful of the pure acid dissolved in half a pint of water. It should be dabbed on the skin with a piece of cotton-wool, three or four times a day.

Sore Throat. Gargle with the carbolic-acid solution as above.

Crushed Finger. Swab with Iodine and cover with gauze dressing. Dress the wound twice a day. If the finger is very badly lacerated it may be necessary to amputate the injured part. If so, clean the finger with spirit and cut through one of the joints with the surgical knife, trying if possible to leave a flap of skin to cover the end of the bone.

VITAMINS

As the average person has a very vague idea of vitamins, it may be as well to give a rough explanation of them.

Natural foods contain certain constituents, the lack of which gives rise to various diseases. They have nothing to do with the digested food; they have no body-building value, neither do they supply any energy. Hence they are called " Accessory Food Factors." They are not present in synthetic foods, no matter how carefully they may have been prepared.

VITAMIN A is comparatively resistant to heat and is present in milk, eggs, cabbages, peas, beans and many other vegetables, also in fat fish and fat meat. An adult can do without this vitamin for a long time, but ultimately the lack of it gives rise to septic complications.

VITAMIN B is resistant to boiling for two hours; it is present in eggs, yeast, potatoes, beans, peas, and many other vegetables. Lack of it gives rise to the disease known as Beri Beri.

VITAMIN C is sensitive to heat and drying. It is present in cabbages, onions, potatoes (raw or cooked), fruit-juices and milk. Dried beans and peas allowed to soak in water and germinate for a few days develop Vitamin C. Lack of this vitamin gives rise to scurvy.

Lime-juice was formerly used to avoid this, and in fact did so, until 1850, when the cordial was made from Mediterranean lemons. Since then, however, West

Indian limes have been used, the juice of which is useless in preventing scurvy.

As potatoes, onions, carrots and eggs will last up to six weeks, the yachtsman need have no worry on the score of vitamins. If the proposed voyage is going to last a longer period, it is advisable to purchase a preparation such as Allen and Hanbury's " Halib-orange," which is a concentrated combination of liver oil and orange-juice.

LIST OF ILLUSTRATIONS

List of Illustrations

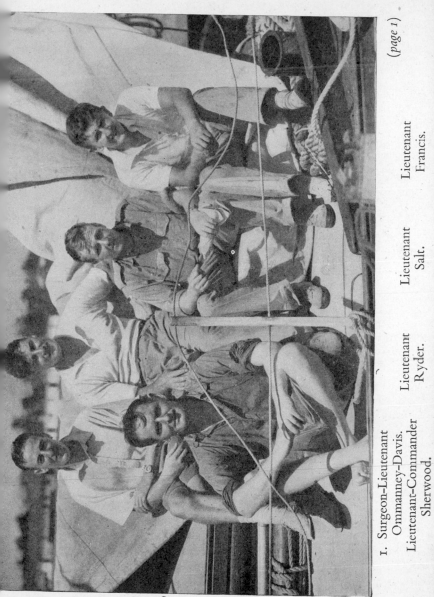

1. Surgeon-Lieutenant   Lieutenant   Lieutenant
   Ommanney-Davis.   Ryder.   Salt.
   Lieutenant-Commander   Lieutenant
   Sherwood.   Francis.

(page 1)

2. " She was then moved out of the shed in which she had been built."
(*page 11*)

3. " On St. George's Day she first floated in her native element."
(*page 12*)

4. " Tai-Mo-Shan is the name of the highest mountain in Hong Kong"

(page 12)

5. " It was surprising how quickly she began to look like the
finished article." (*page 16*)

6. " Our 7-ton keel ... It was cast in one of the shops and bolted on."
(*page 16*)

7. Work up aloft.

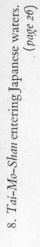

8. *Tai-Mo-Shan* entering Japanese waters.
(page 26)

9. " The conditions were made more complicated by rough weather."
(*page 35*)

10. The Doctor on Watch.

11. The Helmsman was well protected.

12. Ryder, the Navigator.

13. A heavy sea north of Japan.

14. " The vessel lay quite comfortably about six points off the wind."
(*page 58*)

15. " A typhoon which had passed up into the Bering Sea." (*page 59*)

16. Attu—" the perfect model village." *(page 60)*

17. " Deep drifts of snow still remained." *(page 60)*

18. " Sailing in these northern latitudes." *(page 71)*

19. " A fly-catcher which was a passenger on board for thirty-six hours."
(*page 100*)

20. " They would alight close at hand, with their great wings outspread
and their feet stretched out in front of them." (*page 85*)

21. The American yacht *Audacious* accompanied us down the west coast.
(*page 106*)

22. The American yacht *Audacious* during calm weather off
Lower California.   (*page 108*)

23. Becalmed. *(page 109)*

24. " Handed spinnaker.   Set headsails." *(page 118)*

25. " A porpoise was firmly harpooned."
(*page 143*)

26. " It was lucky we had a doctor on board who knew where the liver was situated." (*page 143*)

27. The *Tai-Mo-Shan* at Panama   (*page 148*)

28. " We got a thrill out of our passage through the Panama Canal."
(*page 152*)

29. " We did not have to worry about steering her." (*page 152*)

30. An aerial photograph of our start of the Atlantic from Coco Solo, Panama. *(page 154)*

31. Leaving the Fleet Aviation Base, Coco Solo, Panama. *(page 152)*

32. " We navigated with great caution, sounding frequently
with the lead." *(page 160)*

33. " We dropped our anchor outside the reef." *(page 160)*

34. " We secured planks and with these lashed the rudder amidships."
(*page 170*)

35. " Ashore on Crooked Island in the Bahamas." (*page 166*)

36. " On the morning tide we again renewed our efforts with the help of the villagers." *(page 173)*

37. "Helped by the Seventh-Day Adventists, we proceeded to build a breakwater." *(page 179)*

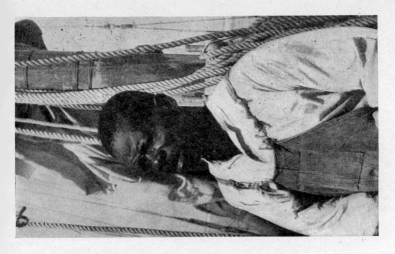

39. "Uncle John." (*page 180*)

38. "They all laughed ; everybody does here." (*page 187*)

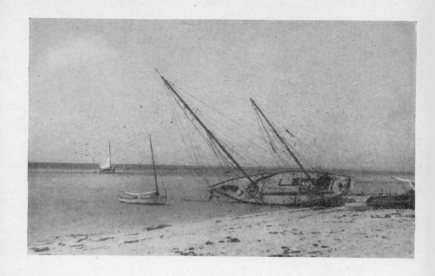

40. " *Tai-Mo-Shan* is facing out to sea." (*page 193*)

41. " We had to work our way out through the passage in the reef."
(*page 197*)

42. " We had to keep the list on the boat."   (*page 197*)

43. " The flagship H.M.S. *Norfolk* was moored alongside the dockyard wall.   We were berthed close astern of her."   (*page 209*)

44. " Logging eight knots."

(*page 219*)

45. *Tai-Mo-Shan* nearing Dartmouth.

(*see p. 000*)

46. " We were accorded a great reception by the Staff and Cadets of the Royal Naval College." (*page 226*)

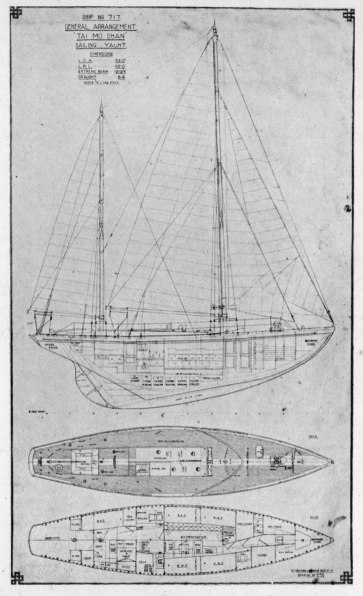

47. General Arrangement. *(page 228)*

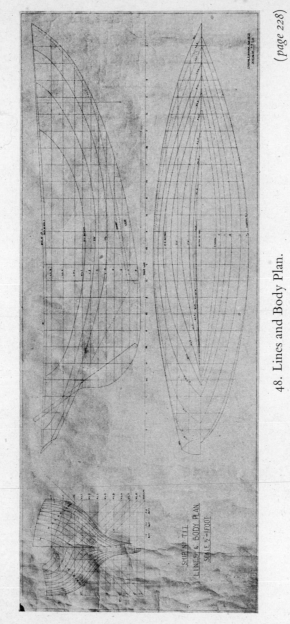

SHIP No. III.
LINES & BODY PLAN.
SCALE ⅛"=1 FOOT.

48. Lines and Body Plan.

(page 228)